INTELLECTUAL PROPERTY AND THE U.S. ECONOMY:
Industries in Focus

Prepared by the

Economics and Statistics Administration

and the

United States Patent and Trademark Office

U.S. Department of Commerce

March 2012

INTELLECTUAL PROPERTY AND THE U.S. ECONOMY:
Industries in Focus

Foreword

As President Obama has said, if we are to win the future and be successful in an increasingly competitive international market, the United States of America must innovate. Innovation, the process through which new ideas are generated and put into commercial practice, is a key force behind U.S. economic growth and national competitiveness. Likewise, U.S. companies' use of trademarks to distinguish their goods and services from those of competitors enables firms to capture market share and further strengthen our economy. The dynamics of a globally connected market mean that the United States will need to develop the brightest minds with the most advanced training to make the best products. The Obama Administration's determination to promote innovation and protect intellectual property (IP) rights will harness the inherent drive and ingenuity of the American people in meeting that goal.

Innovation protected by IP rights is key to creating new jobs and growing exports. Innovation has a positive pervasive effect on the entire economy, and its benefits flow both upstream and downstream to every sector of the U.S. economy. Intellectual property is not just the final product of workers and companies—every job in some way, produces, supplies, consumes, or relies on innovation, creativity, and commercial distinctiveness. Protecting our ideas and IP promotes innovative, open, and competitive markets, and helps ensure that the U.S. private sector remains America's innovation engine.

There is a broad range of industries that benefit from IP, both directly and indirectly, and for every innovation in a given industry, generally there are corresponding economic opportunities for other industries to bring advances to the public. Examples of these complementary industries include the computer manufacturer that uses inputs made by semiconductor firms to make the hardware that is needed to run applications made by software companies, the Internet company that generates the on-line applications to distribute copyrighted music, and the auto manufacturer that incorporates patented energy-saving engines in the cars it sells. In each of these cases, industries are supported by the complementary products and services of another industry, so each industry is in a position to benefit from the safeguard of the IP underpinning their business models. When companies are more confident that their ideas will be protected, they have the incentive to pursue advances that push efficiency forward, costs down, and employment up.

Further evidence of this domino effect is seen as downstream businesses benefit from innovative products that lower their costs and improve their processes and finished articles. For example, a more precise machine could make manufacturing pharmaceuticals safer; a more reliable software program could improve military hardware while making it more affordable; or a clearer sound system could boost the quality of a recording studio's album. In each of these cases, and many more, the innovation feeds directly into a new finished article or service that has commercial value. The innovation may increase customer satisfaction through a higher quality product or service or decrease production costs. This additional value can help businesses protect earnings that can support their labor force.

Finally, in addition to the companies that produce, complement, and consume the innovation, logistical and supporting businesses are required to keep these companies up and running. These entities include marketing firms that inform consumers about innovations that can save time and money, packaging companies that ship advanced goods to retailers, and Internet service providers that create and maintain the communications pathways needed to compete in an increasingly on-line world.

This report by the Economics and Statistics Administration (ESA) and the U.S. Patent and Trademark Office (USPTO) of the U.S. Department of Commerce attempts to identify the first-order players that are growing IP in the U.S. economy and protecting their innovations through patents, trademarks, or copyrights. These IP-intensive industries support tens of millions of jobs and contribute several trillion dollars to our gross domestic product (GDP). This report not only estimates the contributions of these industries to our economy, but also gauges the ripple, or domino, effects they have on employment throughout the economy. They represent the leading edge of our economy that is built on the ingenuity of the American people and their future growth is increasingly dependent on effective protection of IP rights both here and abroad.

Rebecca M. Blank
Acting Deputy Secretary of Commerce
and
Under Secretary for Economic Affairs,
Economics and Statistics Administration

David J. Kappos
Under Secretary for Intellectual Property
and
Director, U.S. Patent and Trademark Office

INTELLECTUAL PROPERTY AND THE U.S. ECONOMY:
Industries in Focus

Economics and Statistics Administration

Rebecca M. Blank
Acting Deputy Secretary of Commerce
and
Under Secretary for Economic Affairs

U.S. Patent and Trademark Office

David J. Kappos
Under Secretary for Intellectual Property
and
Director, U.S. Patent and Trademark Office

JOINT PROJECT TEAM

Mark Doms, *Chief Economist*

Brittany Bond, *Economist*

Jocelyn Burston, *Program Analyst*

David Langdon, *Economist*

Fenwick Yu, *Economist*

Stuart Graham, *Chief Economist*

Galen Hancock, *Economist*

ACKNOWLEDGEMENTS

The Project Team would especially like to thank Victoria Espinel, U.S. Intellectual Property Enforcement Coordinator, for suggesting that we undertake this project and for her assistance. Alis Asadurian from ESA and Gabriel Medeiros from the Bureau of Economic Analysis (BEA) made significant contributions to the report.

The Project Team would also like to thank George McKittrick, David Beede, Pragya Nandini, Sandra Cooke-Hull, and Cassandra Ingram from ESA; Paul Harrison, Jim Hirabayashi, and Camille Barr from USPTO; Chi Mac from the Office of Management and Budget; Mark Dumas, Chris Kask, and Lisa Usher from the Bureau of Labor Statistics, Office of Productivity and Technology; Anna Jacobson, Carol Robbins, and Mary Streitweiser from BEA; Jack Moody from the Census Bureau; and Stephen Siwek from Economists Incorporated.

INTELLECTUAL PROPERTY AND THE U.S. ECONOMY: Industries in Focus

EXECUTIVE SUMMARY

Innovation—the process through which new ideas are generated and successfully introduced in the marketplace—is a primary driver of U.S. economic growth and national competitiveness.[1] Likewise, U.S. companies' use of trademarks to distinguish their goods and services from those of competitors represents an additional support for innovation, enabling firms to capture market share, which contributes to growth in our economy. The granting and protection of intellectual property rights is vital to promoting innovation and creativity and is an essential element of our free-enterprise, market-based system. Patents, trademarks, and copyrights are the principal means used to establish ownership of inventions and creative ideas in their various forms, providing a legal foundation to generate tangible benefits from innovation for companies, workers, and consumers. Without this framework, the creators of intellectual property would tend to lose the economic fruits of their own work, thereby undermining the incentives to undertake the investments necessary to develop the IP in the first place.[2] Moreover, without IP protection, the inventor who had invested time and money in developing the new product or service (sunk costs) would always be at a disadvantage to the new firm that could just copy and market the product without having to recoup any sunk costs or pay the higher salaries required by those with the creative talents and skills. As a result, the benefits associated with American ingenuity would tend to more easily flow outside of the United States.

IP is used everywhere in the economy, and IP rights support innovation and creativity in virtually every U.S. industry. While IP rights play a large role in generating economic growth, little attention has been given to identifying which industries produce or use significant amounts of IP and rely most intensively on these rights. This report begins such an investigation by developing several industry-level metrics on IP use and employing these measures to identify a set of the most IP-intensive industries in the U.S. economy. To develop the industry-level metrics discussed, several databases were used, some of which (for the patent and trademark analyses) are publicly available.[3] In the future, more user-friendly sets of these patent and trademark data will be made available on the U.S. Patent and Trademark Office (USPTO) website.

---

[1] National Economic Council et al. 2011, 7.

[2] Ibid., 11.

[3] See *www.uspto.gov/web/offices/ac/ido/oeip/taf/data/naics_conc/* and also *www.google.com/googlebooks/uspto-trademarks.html.*

This report employs USPTO administrative data to identify the industries that most intensively use the protection offered by patents and trademarks. For copyrights, the report identifies the set of industries primarily responsible for both the creation and production of copyrighted materials. The report then uses standard statistical methods to identify which American industries are the most patent-, trademark-, and copyright-intensive, and defines this subset of industries as "IP-intensive." Using data collected from sources across the U.S. government, the report examines both the important trends and economic characteristics of these highly IP-intensive industries and their meaningful contributions to the U.S. economy. There are several important findings contained in the report.

According to the analysis in this report, the direct and indirect employment in these industries is substantial: Direct employment in the subset of most IP-intensive industries identified in this report amounted to 27.1 million jobs in 2010, while indirect activities associated with these industries provided an additional 12.9 million jobs throughout the economy in 2010, for a total of 40.0 million jobs, or 27.7 percent of all jobs in the economy.

Because all U.S. industries rely on IP to some degree, the statistics reported here for the sectors that use IP most intensively may tend to under-represent the broad impact of IP in the American economy. Moreover, the statistics reported here may not fully reflect the long-run economic benefits and costs of IP in promoting innovation and productivity growth. For example, while this report shows that employment in trademark-intensive industries is almost six times as great as employment in patent-intensive industries, it may be that the kinds of innovation protected by patents play a larger role in driving the long-run growth of productivity throughout the economy.

This report does not contain policy recommendations and is not intended to directly advance particular policy issues. By developing new quantitative measures of IP-intensity by industry, the report aims to promote a better understanding of the industries where IP plays a particularly important role. Although policy issues are not discussed in this report, as a general matter, we note the importance of achieving a balanced system of IP rights that protects inventors and creators from unlawful use of their work while encouraging innovation, competition, and the markets for technology in which IP is transacted. Importantly, using IP rights to support innovation and creativity means recognizing the public domain and limits such as fair use which balance the public's right to use content legally with IP owners' interests.

PRINCIPAL FINDINGS

- The entire U.S. economy relies on some form of IP, because virtually every industry either produces or uses it.

- By focusing on relevant data and various statistical measures, this report identified 75 industries (from among 313 total) as IP-intensive. These IP-intensive industries directly accounted for 27.1 million American jobs, or 18.8 percent of all employment in the economy, in 2010.[4] A substantial share of IP-intensive employment in the United States was in the 60 trademark-intensive industries, with 22.6 million jobs in 2010. The 26 patent-intensive industries accounted for 3.9 million jobs in 2010, while the 13 copyright-intensive industries provided 5.1 million jobs.[5]

■ IP-intensive industries accounted for about $5.06 trillion in value added, or 34.8 percent of U.S. gross domestic product (GDP), in 2010.

■ While IP-intensive industries directly supported 27.1 million jobs either on their payrolls or under employment contracts, these sectors also indirectly supported 12.9 million more supply chain jobs throughout the economy. In other words, every two jobs in IP-intensive industries support an additional one job elsewhere in the economy. In total, 40.0 million jobs, or 27.7 percent of all jobs, were directly or indirectly attributable to the most IP-intensive industries.

■ Due primarily to historic losses in manufacturing jobs, overall employment in IP-intensive industries has lagged other industries during the last two decades. While employment in non-IP-intensive industries was 21.7 percent higher in 2011 than in 1990, overall IP-intensive industry employment grew 2.3 percent over this same period. Because patent-intensive industries are all in the manufacturing sector, they experienced relatively more employment losses over this period, especially during the past decade.   While trademark-intensive industry employment had edged down 2.3 percent by the end of this period, copyright-intensive industries provided a sizeable employment boost, growing by 46.3 percent between 1990 and 2011.

■ Between 2010 and 2011, the economic recovery led to a 1.6 percent increase in direct employment in IP-intensive industries, faster than the 1.0 percent growth in non-IP-intensive industries. Growth in copyright-intensive industries (2.4 percent), patent-intensive industries (2.3 percent), and trademark-intensive industries (1.1 percent) all outpaced gains in non-IP-intensive industries.

■ Jobs in IP-intensive industries pay well compared to other jobs. Average weekly wages for IP-intensive industries were $1,156 in 2010 or 42 percent higher than the $815 average weekly wages in other (non-IP-intensive) private industries. This wage premium nearly doubled from 22 percent in 1990 to 42 percent by 2010. Patent- and copyright-intensive industries have seen particularly fast wage growth in recent years, with the wage premium

---

[4] Using data provided by the Bureau of Labor Statistics' Industry Productivity program, employment covers the sum of payroll jobs, self-employed persons, and unpaid family workers, and totaled 144.2 million jobs in 2010. Because the unit of measure is jobs (as opposed to persons) and because about 5 percent of all workers have more than one job, the total number of jobs is greater than the 139.1 million employed persons in 2010, as estimated from the Current Population Survey (*www.bls.gov/cps*).

[5] Because several industries were found to intensively use both patents and trademarks or copyrights and trademarks, total IP-intensive industry employment is less than the sum of patent-, trademark-, and copyright-intensive industry employment.

in patent-intensive industries increasing from 66 percent in 2005 to 73 percent in 2010, and the premium in copyright-intensive industries rising from 65 percent to 77 percent.

- The comparatively high wages in IP-intensive industries correspond to, on average, the completion of more years of schooling by these workers. More than 42 percent of workers aged 25 and over in these industries in 2010 were college educated, compared with 34 percent on average in non-IP-intensive industries.

- Merchandise exports of IP-intensive industries totaled $775 billion in 2010, accounting for 60.7 percent of total U.S. merchandise exports.

- Data on foreign trade of IP-intensive service-providing industries is limited; however, this report does find that exports of IP-intensive service-providing industries accounted for approximately 19 percent of total U.S. private services exports in 2007.

INTELLECTUAL PROPERTY AND THE U.S. ECONOMY: Industries in Focus

TABLE OF CONTENTS

I. INTRODUCTION

"The key to our success – as it has always been – will be to compete by developing new products, by generating new industries, by maintaining our role as the world's engine of scientific discovery and technological innovation. It's absolutely essential to our future."

– President Barack Obama, November 17, 2010

A defining characteristic of the U.S. economy throughout its history is its rapid and sustained growth. For example, real income per person two hundred years ago was four percent of what it is today.[6] Strong and sustained economic growth results from several factors, but among the most important is innovation, "the process by which individuals and organizations generate new ideas and put them into practice" and create "new and better ways of producing goods and services."[7] Likewise, U.S. companies' use of trademarks to distinguish their goods and services from those of competitors represents an additional support for innovation, enabling firms to capture market share and promoting growth in our economy.

One important way to help encourage innovation is through the protection of intellectual property (IP). The investments necessary to develop IP are often quite substantial. Firms and individuals, in order to invest the necessary resources, need some assurance that they will benefit from and recover the costs of the creation of intellectual property. IP rights help protect authors, inventors, and merchants of goods and services from having their creations and innovations quickly and easily exploited by other firms or individuals, diminishing the benefits to the inventor of the IP. This reduction in private benefits to be gained from the underlying innovation could, in turn, reduce the incentives to undertake the investments necessary to develop the IP in the first place.[8]

Protection of IP has been a critical function of the U.S. government since the founding of this country. Indeed, Article I, Section 8, Clause 8 of the U.S. Constitution grants to Congress the power to "promote the Progress of Science and useful Arts by securing for limited Times to Authors and Inventors the exclusive Right to their respective Writings and Discoveries."

Patents, trademarks, and copyrights are the principal means for establishing ownership rights to inventions and ideas, and they provide a legal foundation by which intangible ideas generate tangible benefits to firms and workers. IP protection affects commerce throughout the economy by:

---

[6] Maddison 2006.

[7] National Economic Council et al. 2011, 7.

[8] Ibid., 11.

- Providing incentives to invent and create;

- Protecting innovators from unauthorized copying;

- Facilitating vertical specialization in technology markets;

- Creating a platform for financial investments in innovation;

- Supporting entrepreneurial liquidity through mergers, acquisitions, and IPOs;

- Making licensing-based technology business models possible; and

- Enabling a more efficient market for technology transfer and trading in technology and ideas.

Certain industries find IP protection to be especially important and consequently register a relatively high number of patents, trademarks, and copyrights compared with other similarly sized industries. Still, as a general matter, we note the importance of achieving a balanced system of IP rights that protects inventors and creators from unlawful use of their work while encouraging innovation, competition, and the markets for technology in which IP is transacted. Importantly, using IP to support innovation and creativity means recognizing the public domain and limits such as fair use which balance the public's right to use content legally with IP owners' interests.

This report, prepared by the Economics and Statistics Administration (ESA) and the U.S. Patent and Trademark Office (USPTO) of the U.S. Department of Commerce, focuses on identifying these IP-intensive industries and examining their characteristics and contributions to the overall economy. Using administrative data and economic literature analyzing IP protection, this report develops various metrics of IP usage by industry. The report does not contain policy recommendations and is not intended to directly advance particular policy issues. By developing new measures of IP-intensity by industry, the report provides a better understanding of the industries where IP plays a particularly important role.

To be specific, the report identifies 75 industries (from among 313 total) that are particularly dependent on patent, copyright, or trademark protection and which we define as IP-intensive. The second section of this report, "Identifying IP-Intensive Industries," lays out the methodologies used to develop these metrics and details which industries were selected as IP-intensive. Given the differing natures of patents, copyrights and trademarks along with data limitations, we developed separate approaches that are consistent, to the extent possible, for identifying which industries rely on patents, trademarks, or copyrights.

In the third section of this report, we present evidence on the size of these industries relative to the economy as a whole. This analysis points to several key results. First, these industries accounted for 27.1 million, or 18.8 percent, of all jobs in 2010.[9] They contributed 34.8 percent to gross domestic product (GDP), with total value added of $5.06 trillion in 2010. The bulk of employment and value added correspond to the 60 trademark-intensive industries, which is a reflection of the nearly ubiquitous use of trademarks and logos in the marketplace. The share of total employment in many IP-intensive industries has edged down over the past two decades. Further, it is important to note that these 75 industries are by no means the only ones with business models and profits supported by IP protection. Indeed, as discussed more below, this report reinforces the notion that all sectors of the economy actively use IP protection.

In addition, we examine how these industries have performed relative to other, less IP-intensive industries. In particular, although IP-intensive industries have not performed as well in job growth relative to other sectors over the last two decades, IP-intensive industries have been a source of high-quality jobs, with average weekly wages in these industries averaging 42 percent higher than the average for all other industries. The workers in IP-intensive industries also tend to be better educated, on average, than other workers: more than 42 percent of workers age 25 and over in these IP-intensive industries were college educated, compared to one in three in other industries. Copyright-intensive industries, in particular, employed the most educated workers, with 61 percent holding at least a college degree. Finally, IP-intensive industries awere large contributors to U.S. foreign trade, accounting for about 60.7 percent of total merchandise exports and about 19 percent of service exports.

---

[9] This analysis uses employment data from the Bureau of Labor Statistics' Industry Productivity program, which includes the sum of payroll jobs, self-employed persons, and unpaid family workers and totaled 144.2 million jobs in 2010. Because the unit of measure is jobs (as opposed to persons) and because about 5 percent of all workers have more than one job, the total number of jobs is greater than the 139.1 million employed persons in 2010, as estimated from the Current Population Survey (*www.bls.gov/cps*).

II. IDENTIFYING IP-INTENSIVE INDUSTRIES

PATENTS

Overview

Utility patents, hereafter referred to as "patents" unless otherwise noted, assist owners in protecting the rights to inventions and innovative processes.[10] A patent issued by the USPTO enables the owner to pursue legal action to exclude "others from making, using, offering for sale, or selling the invention throughout the United States or importing the invention into the United States."[11] U.S. patents are issued to inventors who can assign their ownership rights to individuals, corporations, universities, other organizations, or branches of governments of any nationality.[12, 13] Our patent analysis focuses only on patents issued to U.S corporations, which accounted for about 45 percent of total patents issued between fiscal years (FY) 2004 and 2008 and 87 percent of all U.S.-owned patents for this time period.[14, 15]

Patents are further classified in over 430 patent "technology classes" that distinguish their inventive content.[16] Additionally, the USPTO maintains a general concordance between its technology classifications and 32 North America Industry Classification System (NAICS) codes (26 unique codes and 6 combinations), which enables analysts to associate patents with these industries.[17] We rely on these NAICS-based patent counts for FY 2004 to FY 2008 to identify

---

[10] In addition to utility patents, there are two other types of patents: design and plant. Utility patents apply to processes, machines, articles of manufacture, composition of matter, or any new and useful improvements thereof. Design patents apply to ornamental designs for an article of manufacture. Plant patents apply to the invention or discovery of selected new varieties of asexually reproducing plants.

[11] 35 U.S.C. ß 157(a)(1). This right was established over 200 years ago in fulfillment of Article 1, Section 8 of the United States Constitution: "The Congress shall have Power... To promote the Progress of Science and useful Arts, by securing for limited Times to Authors and Inventors the exclusive Right to their respective Writings and Discoveries;" *www.uspto.gov/patents/index.jsp*.

[12] Inventors, who are always individuals and not organizations, apply for patents. The inventors can transfer (assign) their rights to anyone, including organizations, and can do so before or after the patent is issued. Commonly, inventors work for employers who hire them to create new inventions, and as part of their employment agreements agree in advance to assign to their employers any patent rights that result from their work.

[13] Today, multiple inventors on a single patent often come from several nations, an example of globalization's impact on innovation.

[14] The "U.S. corporation" category of ownership in USPTO reports broadly includes private organizations, including small and large companies, nonprofits, partnerships, and universities.

[15] See Tables A1-1a, A1-1b at *www.uspto.gov/web/offices/ac/ido/oeip/taf/h_at.htm#PartA1_1b*.

[16] Utility patents may be classified into more than one technology class, but are organized according to their primary classification.

[17] This concordance was created by the USPTO with financial support from the National Science Foundation. For an overview of NAICS, see *www.census.gov/eos/www/naics/index.html*.

patent-intensive industries.[18] Just as a patent can be assigned to more than one technology class, it also may be associated with multiple industries. Because no similar concordances to NAICS are available for plant or design patents, only utility patents were used in our analysis.[19] This approach strictly limits the patent analysis to the manufacturing sector because the concordance system only associates patents with manufacturing industries. Service-providing industries may also rely on utility patents in their production processes, but these industries are not captured by the patent-NAICS concordance that we employ.

Fractional vs. Whole Patents Counts

The USPTO reports patent data by NAICS category using two different counting measures. The first gives one full count to every industry associated with a particular patent. The second divides each patent by the number of industries it is associated with, thus creating fractional counts of patents. The sum of the fractional counts equals the total number of patents issued in a given year, while the sum of the whole counts across industries is greater than the number of patents issued. Patent analyses within a given industry or technology class commonly use whole counts; however, cross-industry analyses typically use fractional counts in order to avoid over-counting. For these same reasons, fractional counts are used in this report.[20, 21] It is important to note that the NAICS concordance maintained by the USPTO associates each patent with its final use in the economy. In practice, this means that the patents are all associated with manufacturing NAICS codes regardless of whether the company that owns them is a manufacturer or a company that may be classified in the services sector.[22]

Methodology

The USPTO has NAICS-based patent data covering the period from 1963 to 2008. We calculated a measure of industry patent "intensity," defined as the ratio of total patents over the five years in a NAICS category to the average payroll employment by industry. Because employment is a gauge of industry size, dividing patent counts by employment normalizes patenting activity with respect to industry size.[23] This approach helps put all industries on an even playing field, so that the most patent-intensive industries were defined not as the ones with the most patents, but rather those with the most patents per job.

---

[18] See *www.uspto.gov/web/offices/ac/ido/oeip/taf/data/misc/patenting_trends/info_ptrends2008.txt*.

[19] To contrast the scale of technology patents, design patents break out into 33 classes and plant patents into only one patent class. See *www.uspto.gov/web/offices/ac/ido/oeip/taf/all_tech.htm* for more information on utility patents.

[20] It should be noted that the use of fractional patent counts differs somewhat from our treatment of trademark registrations for which whole counts of registrations by class were used.

[21] As a robustness check, we repeated our analysis using full counts and found little difference in our final results.

[22] For full details on the nature and caveats of the patent data used, see *www.uspto.gov/web/offices/ac/ido/oeip/taf/govt/naics/explan_naics.htm*.

[23] Value added and gross output are two alternative gauges of industry size; however, estimates at the level of detail needed for this analysis are not publicly available due to data confidentiality limitations.

By using a five-year period (in this case, FY 2004-08, the most recent period for which data are available) instead of just one year helps minimize the chance that anomalies in any given year will skew our results. The analysis was performed at the greatest possible level of NAICS industry detail, and so results include four-digit industries as well as some individual three-digit industries and combinations of three- or four-digit industries.[24] As will be seen in the results, most patent-intensive industries in the sample fall into the four-digit NAICS industries, which may be a product of the patent-intensive nature of these more finely disaggregated industry sectors.

Results

We defined patent-intensive industries as ones with above-average patent intensity (patent/job ratio) when comparing all industries.[25] (See Table 1.) The four most patent-intensive industries all have intensity rates that are one standard deviation above the mean patent-intensity cutoff, and are all classified in computer and electronic product manufacturing (NAICS 334). This three-digit NAICS industry includes computer and peripheral equipment; communications equipment; other computer and electronic products; semiconductor and other electronic components; and navigational, measuring, electro-medical, and control instruments. This is unsurprising when one also looks at the recent top ten U.S. companies ranked by granted patents.[26, 27] This group of companies includes Intel, Hewlett-Packard, Micron Technology, and Texas Instruments, each of which is closely associated with computer and computer peripheral manufacturing.

USPTO's Patent Class - NAICS Concordance

The scheme used by the USPTO to associate utility patents with their proper NAICS designation includes groups of four-digit as well as three-digit NAICS codes. With respect to machinery manufacturing (NAICS 333) and electrical equipment, appliance, and component manufacturing (NAICS 335), the USPTO does not provide a breakdown beyond this three-digit level, largely because many of the classes in these categories overlap with other NAICS codes. Thus, our analysis of patents cannot measure patent intensity in NAICS 333 and 335 at a more disaggregated level because technology classes corresponding to these industry categories cannot easily and cleanly be associated with more detailed NAICS industries. Because we cannot disaggregate these two industries, or the groupings of NAICS 3343 and 3346, and NAICS 3253, 3255, and 3256 (which also were found to be patent-intensive) into their four-digit NAICS components, it is not possible to know whether each of the individual four-digit industries is patent-intensive according to our definition.

---

[24] In the NAICS classification, a three-digit code is a larger aggregation as compared to a four-digit code. So, for instance, NAICS 236 "construction of buildings" is a larger aggregation of which NAICS 2361 "residential building construction" is a smaller and more specific subset.

[25] Although we pooled the FY 2004-08 patent counts, we also examined individual years to see how stable the selection of patent-intensive industries would be over time. The list of most intensive industries proves to be relatively stable over time, especially the high rankings of the computer and peripheral equipment manufacturers.

[26] See *www.uspto.gov/web/offices/ac/ido/oeip/taf/asgstc/usa_ror.htm.*

[27] The OneSource Business Browser was used to classify companies to NAICS industries; *www.onesource.com/businessbrowser.aspx.*

Table 1. Patent Intensity, FY 2004-08

	NAICS code	Industry title	Patents (number)	Employment (1000 jobs)	Patent intensity (patents/1000 jobs)
Above mean	3341	Computer and peripheral equipment	54,416	196.1	277.5
	3342	Communications equipment	35,797	135.2	264.8
	3344	Semiconductor and other electronic components	50,088	448.7	111.6
	3343,-6	Other computer and electronic products	7,744	71.4	108.5
	3345	Navigational, measuring, electromedical, and control instruments	42,415	441.3	96.1
	3251	Basic chemicals	12,109	150.9	80.2
	335	Electrical equipment, appliance, and components	23,503	433.0	54.3
	3254	Pharmaceutical and medicines	13,627	291.3	46.8
	3399	Other miscellaneous	12,717	339.2	37.5
	3253,-5,-6,-9	Other chemical products and preparation	10,322	318.1	32.4
	3391	Medical equipment and supplies	9,716	303.2	32.0
	333	Machinery	37,105	1,173.7	31.6
	3252	Resin, synthetic rubber, fibers, and filaments	2,771	106.4	26.0
	326	Plastics and rubber products	8,289	775.8	10.7
	3361-3363	Motor vehicles, trailers and parts	8,298	1,029.8	8.1
	327	Nonmetallic mineral products	3,651	497.2	7.3
	3365,-6,-9	Other transportation equipment	1,585	222.4	7.1
	3364	Aerospace products and parts	2,726	473.3	5.8
	313,-4,-5,-6	Textiles, apparel and leather	2,566	632.2	4.1
	332	Fabricated metal products	5,495	1,532.5	3.6
	331	Primary metals	998	458.9	2.2
	337	Furniture and related products	1,107	543.0	2.0
	322,-3	Paper, printing and support activities	1,313	1102.6	1.2
	312	Beverage and tobacco products	217	195.5	1.1
	321	Wood products	428	527.8	0.8
	311	Food	719	1,483.1	0.5
	Total		354,360	13,882.7	25.5

Source: ESA calculations using data from USPTO and the Bureau of Labor Statistics' Current Employment Statistics program.
Note: The patent count is the total for fiscal years 2004-08, while employment shows the calendar year 2004-08 average in thousands of jobs.

Alternatives and Robustness

The methodology used in this report identifies industries only, and so should not be used to draw conclusions about specific companies in these industries, or in other industries which did not make our list. For example, industries with a relatively small stock of highly valuable patents, but relatively large numbers of employees, would not be selected as patent-intensive in our methodology, even though companies in that industry may rely critically upon patent protection.

The aerospace industry is a good illustration of this point. Its patent-to-jobs ratio was about one-fifth the overall average, but there is other evidence suggesting that patenting is considered important by aerospace companies. In a survey conducted by researchers at Carnegie-Mellon University in 1994, aerospace company R&D managers reported on average that 78 percent of their business units filed for patents (about the same share reported by the pharmaceutical and basic chemical industries, both of which make our list of patent-intensive industries) and that 51 percent of product innovations were being patented (about the same share as in the semiconductor industry, which was also included in our list).[28] So, while it does appear that patenting was relatively important to companies in the aerospace industry during the early 1990s, this sector does not show up in our current list. This outcome could indicate that patent protection is less useful in aerospace than two decades ago (probably unlikely), or it may be an artifact of the manner in which technologies are assigned to industries in our methodology.

Another possibility is that industries may rely on proprietary protections other than patents, such as a trade secret, which may very well be a safer mode of protecting new discoveries in an industry with few competitors monitoring each other closely. Whereas patenting requires disclosure of the details of the new discovery, a trade secret allows the discovery to remain undisclosed, under close in-house protection.

The Carnegie-Mellon University survey allows the consideration of an alternative measure of IP reliance, based not on the number of patents granted per employee, but instead on the responses of research and development (R&D) lab managers to questions concerning the effectiveness of different methods for protecting innovation. Because managers were asked in the survey to report on the percentage of product and process innovations for which patent protection was effective at capturing competitive advantage from the innovation, the study provides a window into the relative importance of patent protection considered against the stock of innovations that industries are producing. As Table 2 makes clear, this survey method results in a different ranking among industries than the patent intensity measures used in this report, with sectors such as pharmaceuticals (drugs), medical equipment, and chemicals ranked most highly.

Because this survey was conducted in the mid 1990s, it was not considered an ideal principal measure for current industry activities. It is noteworthy, however, that the industries reporting that patents were effective for more than 51.0 percent of product innovations and 23.3 percent of process innovations (the overall averages in the survey) are largely the same industries with above-average patent-to-jobs ratios (patent intensity) in the mid-to-late 2000s. For this reason, the Carnegie-Mellon University survey results serve as an important robustness check for the accuracy of the methodology selected in this report for patent-intensive industries.

---

[28] See Cohen et al. 2000.

Table 2. Percent of Product and Process Innovations for which Patents were Considered an Effective Mechanism for Appropriating the Returns to Innovation, by Industry.

SIC code	Industry title	Product innovations (percent)	SIC code	Industry title	Process innovations (percent)
3311	**Medical equipment**	**54.70%**	2320	**Petroleum**	**36.67%**
2423	**Drugs**	**50.20%**	2423	**Drugs**	**36.15%**
2920	**Special purpose machinery, nec.**	**48.83%**	3311	**Medical equipment**	**34.02%**
3430	**Auto parts**	**44.35%**	2700	**Metal, nec.**	**31.67%**
3010	**Computers**	**41.00%**	2610	**Glass**	**30.83%**
2429	**Miscellaneous chemicals**	**39.66%**	3010	**Computers**	**30.25%**
2800	**Metal products**	**39.43%**	2411	**Basic chemicals**	**29.71%**
3410	**Car/truck**	**38.89%**	2920	**Special purpose machinery, nec.**	**28.57%**
2411	**Basic chemicals**	**38.86%**	2100	**Paper**	**27.58%**
2910	**General purpose machinery, nec.**	**38.78%**	2429	**Miscellaneous chemicals**	**27.32%**
3230	**TV/radio**	**38.75%**	1700	**Textiles**	**25.22%**
2400	**Chemicals, nec.**	**37.46%**	3430	**Auto parts**	**24.35%**
2100	**Paper**	**36.94%**	2910	**General purpose machinery, nec.**	**23.62%**
2922	**Machine tools**	**36.00%**	3600	**Other manufacturing**	**23.42%**
3100	Electrical equipment	34.55%	2600	**Mineral products**	**23.33%**
3600	Other manufacturing	33.81%	3210	**Semiconductors and related equipment**	**23.33%**
2320	Petroleum	33.33%	2800	Metal products	22.50%
2413	Plastic resins	32.96%	3110	Motor/generator	22.14%
3530	Aerospace	32.92%	3410	Car/truck	21.67%
2500	Rubber/plastic	32.71%	3530	Aerospace	21.38%
2610	Glass	30.83%	2413	Plastic resins	21.30%
2695	Concrete, cement, lime	30.00%	2400	Chemicals, nec.	20.40%
3314	Search/navigational equipment	28.68%	2500	Rubber/plastic	19.86%
3210	Electronic components	26.67%	3100	Electrical equipment	19.09%
3312	Precision instruments	25.86%	3230	TV/radio	18.75%
3220	Communications equipment	25.74%	2695	Concrete, cement, lime	18.50%
3110	Motor/generator	25.23%	2922	Machine tools	18.00%
2710	Steel	22.00%	3312	Precision instruments	16.77%
3210	Semiconductors and related equipment	21.35%	1500	Food	16.40%
			2710	Steel	15.50%
2600	Mineral products	21.11%	3210	Electronic components	15.19%
1700	Textiles	20.00%	3220	Communications equipment	14.70%
2700	Metal, nec.	20.00%	3314	Search/navigational equipment	13.24%
1500	Food	18.26%			
2200	Printing/publishing	12.08%	2200	Printing/publishing	8.64%
	All industries	**34.83%**		**All industries**	**23.30%**

Source: Cohen et al. 2000, Tables 1 and 2.

Note: Estimates are the mean percentage of product or process innovations for which patents were considered by respondent to be effective for securing competitive advantage. Bolded industries in each list are those with response scores above the industry-level mean for all industries surveyed in the study. Industries are defined according to the 1987 Standard Industrial Classification (SIC) system, the precursor to NAICS. The abbreviation "nec." stands for "not elsewhere classified."

Trademarks

Overview

Industries throughout the economy rely on trademarks registered at the USPTO to protect brands for the goods and services they market.[29] A trademark is "a word, phrase, symbol, or design, or a combination thereof, that identifies and distinguishes the source of the goods of one party from those of others."[30] Unlike a patent, which protects an invention, or a copyright, which protects a work of original authorship, a trademark does not protect a new product or service *per se*. A trademark instead confers protection upon the brand or identity of a good, thus preventing competitors from leveraging another firm's reputation and confusing consumers as to the source of the goods. Service marks are similar in nature to trademarks, but distinguish the source of a service rather than a good.[31] In the remainder of this text, the term "trademark" will refer to both trademarks and service marks.

Any company or individual, American or foreign, can apply to register a trademark with the USPTO for a nominal fee. Once granted, trademark registrations can remain in force indefinitely as long as the trademark remains in active use and maintenance payments are made. If the trademark is not in active use and maintained, the rights will cease after a period of time, normally five years. To maintain trademark registrations, new owners must file a Section 8 Affidavit of Continuous Use before the end of the sixth year after the initial registration date. Trademark registrations must be renewed on or about every 10-year anniversary of the registration of the trademark.[32]

Identifying Trademark-Intensive Industries

Unlike patents, there is little academic research examining industry use of trademarks. Accordingly, this report offers what may be the first comprehensive analysis of trademark use by U.S. industries that is grounded in original research, data, and measurement theory. As a preliminary matter, we recognized that each trademark registration has a description of the type of good or service with which the protected mark is used in commerce. The USPTO classifies goods and services for administrative convenience, and applicants for trademark registration must provide a separate description—and pay separate application and maintenance fees—for

---

[29] We note that trademark owners are not required to register their trademarks. Parties can acquire rights in their trademarks merely by using those trademarks. In addition, trademark owners who wish to register their trademark may do so not only at the USPTO, but with state authorities as well, or with both. The trademarks that were analyzed in connection with the present study were all registered at the USPTO.

[30] USPTO 2010a.

[31] For example, the Whole Foods Market grocery store brand name is a service mark for retail grocery store services, and also a trademark for hair shampoo and soap.

[32] There is no further 6-year affidavit requirement after the first 10-year term. Overall, 46 percent of the nearly 822,000 registrations from the 1990s "survived" into the 2000s.

each "class" in which the goods or services associated with the trademark is classified.[33] This makes working with trademark registration data different from working with patent grant data.

Trademark application and maintenance fees are assessed on a per-class basis, and registration holders may elect to renew their registrations with respect to some but not all classes. As a result, holding a "multi-class" registration is practically equivalent to holding multiple registrations, one for each class. Accordingly, in the foregoing analysis each class listed on a registration was considered as the unit of analysis, creating a class-registration count. For example, if one mark (or logo) is registered in three classes, then our input measure in the analysis reflects three trademark registration counts, one for each class.[34]

In practice, the vast majority of trademark registrations are associated with a single class. However, from 2000 to 2009, about 16 percent of trademarks were registered in more than one class. About 10 percent were registered in two classes, while the remaining six percent were registered in anywhere from three to 45 classes. As a result of this variation, the sum of registration-class observations is somewhat greater than the sum of registrations.[35]

As an example of a firm that has chosen to register a trademark in multiple classes, consider Whole Foods' "365 Everyday Value" brand. Whole Foods protects the 365 Everyday Value brand in 10 different trademark classes.[36] The goods classes under which the 365 Everyday Value logo is applied include processed foods (from frozen dinners to trail mix), staple foods (cereal, tortilla chips, pasta sauce, cookies), as well as food storage containers, paper products (paper towels and coffee filters), and cosmetics and cleaning preparations (laundry detergent, shampoo, bath gels). In effect, these 10 classes are 10 distinct registrations, each of which can be renewed, or not, separately.

The approach that we adopted for measuring trademark-intensive industries parallels, but differs from, the approach employed when analyzing patents.[37] For patents, each patent was counted only once overall; for trademark measurements, each mark is counted once for each class in which it belongs, potentially counting it more than once overall according to the number of classes in which it is registered. Since it is not easy to ascertain which trademark class-registrations are relatively more important, we used the best measure available, based on the

---

[33] For a list of classes, see Trademark Manual of Examining Procedure (TMEP) chapter 1400 (7th ed. 2010). Fees also are a function of the type of application form used. For more information on the trademarking process, see USPTO 2010a.

[34] An example is the mark "Nike" being registered in classes associated with (a) software, (b) golf equipment, and (c) eyewear. See U.S. trademark registration numbers 3406594, 3389746, and 3081688, each by Nike, Inc.

[35] Another way to think about this is to consider the registration counts to be weighted by the number of classes. So, if the mark for brand A is registered in a single class and the mark for brand B is registered in five classes, then, we calculate total registrations = Σ (classes per mark$_{\text{brand i}}$ * mark$_{\text{brand i}}$) = (1*1) + (5*1) = 6.

[36] This trademark is serial number 76977931 and can be found by using the USPTO searchable trademark database at *tarr.uspto.gov/servlet/tarr?regser=serial&entry=76977931*.

[37] For example, the list of industries selected because of their trademark intensity, as described in the next section, includes 55 industries. Had we calculated the intensities based on fractional trademark counts, the list would have numbered 51 industries, with 49 industries appearing on both lists.

economic realities of the fee system.[38] Because each trademark class registration involves some fixed filing fee paid to the USPTO, the more classes in which a trademark is registered indicate more times that a fee has been paid to the USPTO. Using these fee-payments is an effective method to base an IP-intensity measure and this approach was followed consistently for both trademarks and patents. Also, as a sensitivity measure, we found that counting patents and trademarks differently, by using whole counts for patents for example, produced similar results.

Because trademark registrations can be segmented by class but not by industry, there is no USPTO NAICS concordance for these data. Due to this methodological limitation, there is no single, straightforward way to tabulate registrations and measure trademark intensities by industry. Accordingly, and because the measurement of trademark use is a new science, we opted for over-inclusiveness and developed a three-pronged approach to identifying trademark-intensive industries.

We relied on three related but distinct approaches, using different samples of companies that have registered USPTO trademarks. The first approach is the closest approximation to the methodology used to identify patent-intensive industries. Starting with the complete set of trademark registrations, we matched publicly traded companies by their name to a separate database containing information on the firms' primary industry and number of employees. These data allowed us to calculate trademark intensities by industry for the matched firms. In the second approach, we reviewed lists of the top 50 corporate trademark registrants published by the USPTO (which, unlike the first approach, include both private and public companies) and identified industries that appear repeatedly. To help moderate the tendency of the first two approaches to under-represent smaller and younger firms, our third approach focused on a representative and random sample of firms drawn from the complete database of U.S. corporate trademark registrations from FY 2004 to FY 2008.

Trademark Intensities

Methodology

Parallel to our method for defining patent intensities, we defined trademark intensities as the ratio of trademark registrations to employment in a given industry. Thus, we measured the number of trademark registrations per employee. The USPTO applied a firm-name standardization routine developed originally for patent analysis in order to match companies with new trademark registrations to companies in Compustat's database of financial statements of publicly traded companies.[39] This matching identified 386,998 distinct standardized firm names in the FY 2004-08 trademark registration and trademark renewal records. These were firms that either registered or renewed at least one trademark from FY 2004 to FY 2008. These records were matched with 9,539 parent-company records drawn from the Compustat database.

---

[38] We could weight companies by number of employees, but it is more difficult to decide whether a given trademark taken by itself should be weighted heavily or lightly.

[39] This methodology has previously been applied in studies of patents, particularly as detailed in Hall, Jaffe, and Trajtenberg 2001. This paper and other supporting documentation are available at *www.nber.org/patents/*.

Successful matches were made for 3,475 firms. Since Compustat records also include NAICS codes, it was straightforward to sum trademark registrations and employment by four-digit NAICS industry and then estimate industry trademark intensity as the number of matched firm trademarks per worker in each industry.[40]

Because Compustat does not record the relationships between parent and subsidiary companies, the identities of trademark registrants were only matched to the name of the publicly traded parent company reporting financial statements to the U.S. government. Accordingly, trademarks registered in the name of subsidiaries that have different names than the parent company were not matched by this method.[41]

Results

Overall, this procedure identified 235 four-digit NAICS industries with trademark registrations among publicly traded parent companies. The employment-weighted mean trademark intensity for these firms was 1.86 trademarks per 1,000 workers, and the weighted standard deviation was 3.80. Upon examining this distribution, we defined as trademark-intensive the 55 industries with trademark intensities above the sample industry mean, consistent with our approach for identifying patent-intensive industries. We also set as a minimum a sample size in each four-digit NAICS industry of five distinct firms and 100 registrations over the 5-year period. These minima helped us avoid wrongly selecting as trademark-intensive any industries that had high estimated trademark intensities but very few firms in the matched sample or very low absolute trademark registration activity.

As shown in Table 3, the 55 industries span most major industry sectors, with many industries in the manufacturing and information sectors, as well as others from the financial activities, professional and technical services, mining, construction, healthcare, and leisure and hospitality sectors. Four industries stood out from the rest due to their notably high trademark intensities: audio and video equipment manufacturing (82.5 trademarks per 1,000 employees), other miscellaneous manufacturing (64.5), satellite telecommunications (35.3), and lessors of nonfinancial intangible assets (33.3). The first two industries also ranked above the mean in our patent-intensive listing. The category "lessors of nonfinancial intangible assets" is a special case. That industry's sole function is to assign "rights to assets, such as patents, trademarks, brand names, and/or franchise agreements [but not to copyrighted works] for which a royalty payment or licensing fee is paid to the asset holder."[42] Thus, the industry is by definition IP-

---

[40] To the extent that matched firms differ in their trademarking behavior relative to unmatched firms, these trademark intensities are biased. However, what really matters for our analysis is not whether the estimates are individually biased but rather if any bias varies across industries.

[41] For this reason, this method not only tends to overweight large, publicly traded companies, but also those companies that have a particular trademark-registration approach. Although no studies to our knowledge have been done on the practices of corporate trademark registration at the parent or subsidiary level, recent patent scholarship suggests that IP ownership may show systematic differences along these dimensions. See Arora, Belenzon, and Rios 2011, 29-30.

[42] See *www.census.gov/cgi-bin/sssd/naics/naicsrch?code=533110&search=2007*, noting that six-digit NAICS industry 533110 and four-digit NAICS industry 5331 are identical. The entire 2007 NAICS manual can be found online at *www.census.gov/eos/www/naics/index.html.*

intensive, but could not be selected as patent-intensive because all patents were assigned by the USPTO NAICS concordance only to manufacturing industries.

Table 3. Industries with Above-Average Trademark Intensity, FY 2004-08

NAICS code	Industry title	Trademark intensity (trademarks/ 1000 workers)	NAICS code	Industry title	Trademark intensity (trademarks/ 1000 workers)
3343	Audio & video equipment mfg.	82.5	3231	Printing & related support activities	3.6
3399	Other miscellaneous manufacturing	64.5	5416	Management & technical consulting	3.5
5174	Satellite telecommunications	35.3	3345	Electronic instrument mfg.	3.4
5331	Lessors of nonfinancial intangible assets	33.3	5241	Insurance carriers	3.4
5191	Other information services	14.8	4234	Commercial equip. merchant wholesalers	3.1
5615	Travel arrangement & reservation	13.5	3115	Dairy product manufacturing	3.0
5179	Other telecommunications	12.4	3222	Converted paper product mfg.	2.9
5311	Lessors of real estate	11.2	3251	Basic chemical manufacturing	2.9
5112	Software publishers	8.2	4511	Sporting goods, hobby, and musical instrument stores	2.9
4541	Electronic shopping & mail-order houses	7.7	3121	Beverage manufacturing	2.8
3256	Soap, cleaning compound, & toiletries	7.4	5614	Business support services	2.7
3322	Cutlery & handtool manufacturing	7.3	3221	Pulp, paper, & paperboard mills	2.6
			3252	Resin, rubber, & artificial fibers	2.6
3339	Other general purpose machinery manufacturing	6.1	3261	Plastics product manufacturing	2.6
3391	Medical equipment & supplies manufacturing	5.9	3259	Other chemical product & preparations	2.5
5111	Newspaper, book, & directory publishers	5.8	4242	Druggists' goods merchant wholesalers	2.5
3333	Commercial & service industry manufacturing	5.4	3353	Electrical equipment mfg.	2.4
5417	Scientific research & development	5.4	6214	Outpatient care centers	2.4
3359	Other electrical equipment & components	4.7	5239	Other financial investment activities	2.3
3254	Pharmaceutical & medicine mfg.	4.6	7132	Gambling industries	2.3
3162	Footwear manufacturing	4.4	3112	Grain & oilseed milling	2.2
5121	Motion picture & video industries	4.3	3336	Turbine & power transmission equipment	2.2
3371	Household & institutional furniture	4.2	5152	Cable & other subscription programming	2.2
			3119	Other food manufacturing	2.0
4244	Grocery & related product wholesalers	4.1	3329	Other fabricated metal product manufacturing	1.9
2361	Residential building construction	4.0	3341	Computer & peripheral equipment	1.9
3352	Household appliance manufacturing	3.8			
2111	Oil & gas extraction	3.7	5221	Depository credit intermediation	1.9
3332	Industrial machinery manufacturing	3.7			
3342	Communications equipment mfg.	3.7			

Source: USPTO calculations using the agency's trademark registration data and company employment data from Compustat.

Top 50 Trademark-Registering Companies

Methodology

Since 2006, the USPTO's annual *Fiscal Year Performance and Accountability Reports* have identified the 50 companies that obtained the largest number of trademark registrations during the Federal fiscal year.[43] Because these reports do not provide the primary NAICS code of the companies in question, we used OneSource, a subscription-based dataset, to determine the relevant NAICS industry classification for each of the companies listed for FY 2006-10.[44, 45] On the theory that these large companies operate in industries with large numbers of trademark registrations relative to the size of the industry, a subset of those industries was defined as trademark-intensive.

After assigning each company to a four-digit NAICS industry, we tabulated the number of times each industry appeared in the top 50 during the FY 2006-10 period. We designated industries as trademark-intensive if they had counts of five or higher. At the extremes, counts of five or higher occurred if a given company was among the top 50 registrants in each of the five years studied, or if five different companies in an industry had reached the top 50 in a single year during the period. The tabulations showed neither of those extremes. Two industries were selected based on their score of five—sugar and confectionary products (NAICS 3113) and household appliances (3352)—and in both cases, two or more companies accounted for the top 50 trademark registrations.

Results

There are 14 industries with counts of five or greater, with other miscellaneous manufacturing at the top with 32.[46] (See Table 4.) Also scoring in the double-digits are pharmaceutical and medicine manufacturing; soap, cleaning compound, and toiletry product manufacturing; and

---

[43] See *www.uspto.gov/about/stratplan/ar/index.jsp* to access the annual "Performance and Accountability Reports." In each report, the Top 50 Trademark Registrants tables are Table 29B within the USPTO Workload Tables in section 5, "Other Accompanying Information."

[44] This subscription-based dataset is available online at *businessbrowser.onesource.com/homepage.aspx*.

[45] As the results will highlight, classifying a company into a single NAICS industry is not straightforward. Generally, this report used the OneSource entry for the parent company of the firm in the top 50 listing to assign an industry code. The exceptions were when a company did not appear in OneSource and when the listed firm's industry differed considerably from the parent company's industry. As an example of the latter case, Bath & Body Works is a health and personal care store (NAICS 4461) even though its parent company Limited Brands, Inc. is classified under clothing stores (NAICS 4481). Other publicly available data were used to classify companies not included in OneSource.

[46] Toys, jewelry, sporting goods, pencils, signs, musical instruments, buttons, and caskets, among other goods, are some of the product lines in the miscellaneous manufacturing industry. Games and toys, however, are what dominate the trademarking activity for this NAICS code, as Hasbro, Mattel, International Game Technology, and WMS Gaming are each classified within "Other miscellaneous manufacturing." These four companies account for 18 of the 32 appearances for this NAICS code in the top 50 lists.

motion picture and video industries.[47] The industries that were selected using this approach further validated the trademark-intensity approach, as 10 of the 14 industries identified here were also flagged based on their trademark intensity. The four additional industries are sugar and confectionary product manufacturing, motor vehicle manufacturing, grocery stores, and radio and television broadcasting.

Table 4. Industries with Five or More Appearances in the Listings of Top 50 Trademark Registering Companies, FY 2006-10

NAICS code	Industry title	Number of Top 50 appearances
3399	Other miscellaneous manufacturing	32
3254	Pharmaceutical and medicine manufacturing	30
3256	Soap, cleaning compound, and toiletry product manufacturing	29
5121	Motion picture and video industries	14
5111	Newspaper, periodical, book, and directory publishers	9
5151	Radio and television broadcasting	9
5241	Insurance carriers	7
3343	Audio and video equipment manufacturing	7
3121	Beverage manufacturing	7
7132	Gambling industries	6
4451	Grocery stores	6
3361	Motor vehicle manufacturing	6
3352	Household appliance manufacturing	5
3113	Sugar and confectionery product manufacturing	5

Source: ESA calculations using data from the USPTO Annual Reports, Table 29B and OneSource.

---

[47] Three companies were responsible for the bulk of the top 50 trademark registrations in the motion picture and video industry: Twentieth Century Fox, Warner Brothers, and World Wrestling Entertainment. The fact that these three companies are classified principally in the motion picture and video industry helps illustrate the difficulty of summarizing large enterprises' activities within a single industry code.

Random Sample of Trademark Registrations

Methodology

One shortcoming of identifying industries based on the trademark intensities or top 50 appearances is that these approaches tend to bias selection toward larger companies that register a greater number of trademarks. Moreover, these approaches can fail to account for the critical importance that single trademarks may hold for large entities (for instance, Coca-Cola soft drinks) or differences in industry composition and concentration. These methods also can miss industries composed of smaller companies that may account for many trademarks as a group but do not otherwise fall in the USPTO top 50 listing. To help overcome these shortcomings, we supplemented the analyses with a random sample of registrants drawn from the universe of all 166,844 trademarks registered in FY 2010. These data were generated by USPTO using publicly available source data.[48] They comprise all 106,560 trademark registrants, both corporate and individual, including company/person name and number of trademarks registered in that year. To measure the industry share of total registered trademarks, a random sample of 300 registrations was drawn from this dataset. U.S. companies were listed as the registrant on 196 of these 300 trademark registrations, or about two-thirds.[49] We assigned four-digit NAICS industry codes to these firms using the same procedure employed for the top 50 corporate registrants.[50] Although limited in size, the sample's industry distribution reinforces the breadth and depth of trademarking activity seen in the other data highlighted throughout this report.

One limitation of this approach is that the sample was drawn from records that pertain to only a single year. This may result in the under-identification of industries that generally register frequently in an average year, but, for some reason, were less active in 2010. The sample size is another important limitation. The sample we used was small because assigning NAICS codes to each company requires the use of many resources. In an ideal data world, the USPTO trademark registry would include each corporate registrant's NAICS code; however, such information is not provided in trademark applications and therefore is not included in the USPTO database. The process of assigning NAICS codes to companies was especially cumbersome because many of the firms drawn from the sample were small businesses with few employees and little publicly available information from which to find or infer a NAICS classification.

---

[48] See USPTO Bulk Data available at *www.google.com/googlebooks/uspto.html*.

[49] This analysis was restricted to U.S.-owned firms because of the great difficulty in assigning NAICS codes to small, foreign-owned firms.

[50] Because the sample was drawn by registrations as opposed to registrants, a single individual or company could be drawn more than once. One company was selected twice in the sample, and so the 196 registrations corresponded to 195 firms.

Results

Table 5 below lists the NAICS industries as well as the share of registrations within the sample for all industries with at least five registrations that were drawn from the sample. We recognize that setting the limit at five registrations is somewhat arbitrary. Because there were no natural breaks in the sample distribution of trademark registrations, we chose this cutoff because it was two standard deviations above the mean and thus a relatively high bar. The seven industries listed in Table 5 account for one-fifth of trademark registrations from the 196 U.S. companies in our sample. Consistent with the list of trademark-intensive industries selected thus far, the ones selected based on the sample span a number of major industry sectors, including manufacturing, retail trade, wholesale trade, and professional and business services. Furthermore, six of the seven selected industries had already been selected as trademark-intensive based on their trademark intensities. The sole addition is clothing stores, which was one of the two NAICS categories with the highest share of registrations in the sample; the other was management, scientific, and technical consulting services. The selection of these seven industries will be further reinforced through a review of corporate brand rankings and trademark class data.

Table 5. Percent Distribution of Trademark Registrations of Selected Industries from Sample of U.S.-Owned, Trademark-Registrant Companies, Ranked by Percent, FY 2010

NAICS code	Industry title	Percent
4481	Clothing stores	3.5%
5416	Management, scientific, and technical consulting services	3.5%
3121	Beverage manufacturing	2.5%
4234	Professional and commercial equipment and supplies merchant wholesalers	2.5%
4511	Sporting goods, hobby, and musical instrument stores	2.5%
5112	Software publishers	2.5%
5417	Scientific research and development services	2.5%

Source: ESA calculations using trademark registration data provided by USPTO and OneSource.

Identifying Trademark-Intensive Industries

This combined approach for determining trademark intensity by industry—and any comprehensive examination of the USPTO trademark registration database—shows that a wide range of industries use trademarks in commerce. This fact maps onto our everyday experience, in which trademarks, brands, and logos are ubiquitous in the marketplace. The results also show that the latter two approaches tend to complement the first approach. The first approach is the most data intensive, and relies on a systematic matching of the entire U.S. trademark registration dataset over a five-year period to a comprehensive dataset of all publicly traded companies in the U.S. Nevertheless, it has limitations, as it may undercount some industries and smaller companies, either because a single trademark in an industry that is highly concentrated may be underrepresented (for instance, Coca-Cola and Pepsi-Cola) or because many small companies are not publicly traded. While the second and third approaches were meant to mitigate these shortcomings, it is interesting to note that there was substantial correlation in the results, with the majority of industries chosen in these two methods also being selected using the criteria in the first analysis. Nevertheless, our intention to capture a broad swath of trademark-intensive industries and the recognition that there were conceptual shortcomings in each approach has led us to treat all three approaches as complementary, and to define as trademark-intensive any industry identified by any of the three approaches. As will be detailed, the final results are broadly corroborated by a separate review of trademark class data and corporate brand rankings.

Table 6 shows the complete list of 60 trademark-intensive industries, which again are defined as any four-digit NAICS industry that is selected based on any one of the three methods: trademark intensity, top 50 registrants, or trademark registration sample. All but five of the industries listed in Table 6 were selected based on their above-average trademark intensity. The five additional industries were selected based on either their top 50 registrations or the trademark registration sample. Only one industry, beverage manufacturing (NAICS 3121), was selected through all three methods.

Table 6. Trademark-Intensive Industries and Selection Criteria

NAICS code	Industry title	Selection criteria		
		Trademark intensity	Top 50	Sample
2111	Oil and gas extraction	X		
2361	Residential building construction	X		
3112	Grain and oilseed milling	X		
3113	Sugar and confectionery product manufacturing		X	
3115	Dairy product manufacturing	X		
3119	Other food manufacturing	X		
3121	Beverage manufacturing	X	X	X
3162	Footwear manufacturing	X		
3221	Pulp, paper, and paperboard mills	X		
3222	Converted paper product manufacturing	X		
3231	Printing and related support activities	X		
3251	Basic chemical manufacturing	X		
3252	Resin, rubber, and artificial fibers	X		
3254	Pharmaceutical and medicine manufacturing	X	X	
3256	Soap, cleaning compound, and toiletries	X	X	
3259	Other chemical product and preparations	X		
3261	Plastics product manufacturing	X		
3322	Cutlery and handtool manufacturing	X		
3329	Other fabricated metal product manufacturing	X		
3332	Industrial machinery manufacturing	X		
3333	Commercial and service industry manufacturing	X		
3336	Turbine and power transmission equipment	X		
3339	Other general purpose machinery manufacturing	X		
3341	Computer and peripheral equipment	X		
3342	Communications equipment manufacturing	X		
3343	Audio and video equipment manufacturing	X	X	
3345	Electronic instrument manufacturing	X		
3352	Household appliance manufacturing	X	X	
3353	Electrical equipment manufacturing	X		
3359	Other electrical equipment and components	X		
3361	Motor vehicle manufacturing		X	

Table 6. Trademark-Intensive Industries and Selection Criteria—Continued

NAICS code	Industry title	Selection criteria		
		Trademark intensity	Top 50	Sample
3371	Household and institutional furniture	X		
3391	Medical equipment and supplies manufacturing	X		
3399	Other miscellaneous manufacturing	X	X	
4234	Commercial equip. merchant wholesalers	X		X
4242	Druggists' goods merchant wholesalers	X		
4244	Grocery and related product wholesalers	X		
4451	Grocery stores		X	
4481	Clothing stores			X
4511	Sporting goods and musical instrument stores	X		X
4541	Electronic shopping and mail-order houses	X		
5111	Newspaper, book, and directory publishing	X	X	
5112	Software publishers	X		X
5121	Motion picture and video industries	X	X	
5151	Radio and television broadcasting		X	
5152	Cable and other subscription programming	X		
5174	Satellite telecommunications	X		
5179	Other telecommunications	X		
5191	Other information services	X		
5221	Depository credit intermediation	X		
5239	Other financial investment activities	X		
5241	Insurance carriers	X	X	
5311	Lessors of real estate	X		
5331	Lessors of nonfinancial intangible assets	X		
5416	Management and technical consulting	X		X
5417	Scientific research and development	X		X
5614	Business support services	X		
5615	Travel arrangement and reservation	X		
6214	Outpatient care centers	X		
7132	Gambling industries	X	X	

Source: ESA and USPTO calculations.

Brands

Firms with high-value brands are likely to seek protection for those brands through trademark law. To check robustness of the methodology for selected trademark-intensive industries, we examined the Interbrand listing of the "Best Global Brands in 2010," focusing on the extent to which firms with highly valued corporate brands operate in industries that have been identified as trademark-intensive.[51]

Methodology

Briefly, Interbrand's methodology for ranking global brands considers the ongoing investment and management of the brand as a business asset.[52] Three key aspects contribute to the assessment of each brand:

- *Financial performance* measures an organization's raw financial return to the investors.

- *Role of brand* measures the portion of the decision to purchase that is attributable to brand.

- *Brand strength* measures the ability of the brand to secure the delivery of expected future earnings.

Before discussing the brand rankings, it is important to review caveats and differences in scope between Interbrand's approach and our approach for identifying trademark-intensive industries. To be included in Interbrand's ranking, companies must have corporate brands that are truly "global, visible, and relatively transparent." First, the company must be present on at least three continents, including "broad coverage in growing and emerging markets." At least 30 percent of revenues must be from outside of the home country, with no more than 50 percent from any single continent. Second, the brand's public profile must extend beyond its own marketplace. Third, firms must prove their profitability through publicly available financial data. These criteria are restrictive relative to the rest of this report, in which the general focus is on all corporations, regardless of their global presence or profits.

Also, it should be emphasized that "brand" refers to single corporate brands as opposed to product brands. This distinction led Interbrand to exclude pharmaceutical companies, which are considered better identified through specific products than the companies themselves. Similarly, Wal-Mart is excluded not because it is insufficiently global as a company, but because it does not operate under a single Wal-Mart brand globally.[53]

The corporate brands included in Interbrand's Best Global Brands are identified by company name, and we assigned four-digit NAICS codes to each listed company using OneSource,

---

[51] Corporate brand generally is equivalent to company name (with its corresponding protected logo), as opposed to a specific product brand, with some exceptions, such as Sprite and Budweiser.

[52] Interbrand 2011a.

[53] Wal-Mart does top the separate rankings of the best retail brands in 2011. See Interbrand 2011b.

following the same methodology we used to assign NAICS codes to the top 50 trademark registrants.[54] We then compared the industries with top-ranked brands with the industries selected as trademark-intensive.

Results

We discovered considerable overlap between the trademark-intensive industries and those with high-ranking brands. Upon assigning NAICS codes to each brand, we calculated that the top 100 ranked brands corresponded to 41 different four-digit NAICS industries, and 24 of these industries (covering 70 brands) were selected as trademark-intensive. Put another way, 24 of the 60 trademark-intensive industries also had high-ranking brands either in the United States or abroad.

Table 7 lists the 24 trademark-intensive industries in which 70 of the various top 100 brands operate.[55] Beverage manufacturing (NAICS 3121) was the most heavily represented industry on the list, with 11 of the top 100 brands—including Coca-Cola, Interbrand's #1 ranked global brand, as well as Pepsi (#23), Budweiser (#30), Sprite (#61), Jack Daniel's (#80), and six foreign brands.[56] This industry is noteworthy because it also was the only one to be selected as trademark-intensive based on all three measures.

While there is much overlap between the trademark-intensive industries and the top-ranked brands, there also were 17 industries that were not considered trademark-intensive based on any of our three measures. Several happened to be among the top 10 brands, including IBM (#2, NAICS 5415), McDonald's (#4, NAICS 7222), General Electric (#5, NAICS 5222), and Intel (#7, NAICS 3344). Nonetheless, these brands are captured to some extent elsewhere in the report. IBM and Intel operate in industries that are found to be copyright- and patent-intensive industries, respectively. General Electric, like a number of the companies examined in this report, operates in various industries. Although its consumer finance arm is in an industry that is not found to be trademark-intensive, other parts of the company are in trademark-intensive industries, such as turbine and power transmission equipment (NAICS 3336). The food service industry, such as limited-service eating places (NAICS 7222), is not captured by

---

[54] The difficulty of assigning a single NAICS code to companies is further highlighted in our analysis of these companies. Take, for example, General Electric, which as described in OneSource is a "diversified technology, media and financial services company... [with] products and services includ[ing] aircraft engines, power generation, water processing, security technology, medical imaging, business and consumer financing, media content and industrial product." No one NAICS code can capture GE. In terms of sales, GE Capital is largest of the company's five principal segments, accounting for 32 percent of total revenue in calendar year 2010, and by this criteria, it makes sense to classify GE in nondepository credit intermediation (NAICS 5222). Still, this does miss the fact that the vast majority of GE's revenues is from other sectors. Two of those sectors, interestingly, also cover industries selected as trademark-intensive. The NBC Universal business segment operates in radio and television broadcasting (NAICS 5151) while part of the Home & Business Solutions segment includes household appliance manufacturing (NAICS 3352). Together these two segments account for 17 percent of total revenue. It should be noted that this discussion applies to data prior to GE's sale of NBC Universal to Comcast.

[55] For a complete listing of Interbrand's top 100 Global Brands, see Interbrand 2011a.

[56] Although Budweiser is part of Anheuser-Busch InBev N.V., which is based in Leuven, Belgium, Interbrand considers the Budweiser brand to be American.

any of the trademark-intensive measures or elsewhere in this report. This is not to say that trademarks or other forms of IP protection are unimportant for protecting food-service industry brands, four of which are in the top 100.

Table 7. Trademark-Intensive Industries with Top 100 Global Brands in 2011

NAICS code	Industry title	Brand		
2111	Oil and gas extraction	Shell		
3112	Grain and oilseed milling	Kellogg's		
3115	Dairy product manufacturing	Nestle	Danone	
3121	Beverage manufacturing	Coca-Cola Budweiser Moet and Chandon Smirnoff Heineken	Pepsi Sprite Johnnie Walker	Nescafe Jack Daniel's Corona
3162	Footwear manufacturing	Nike	Adidas	
3222	Converted paper product manufacturing	Kleenex		
3254	Pharmaceutical and medicine manufacturing	Johnson and Johnson		
3256	Soap, cleaning compound, and toiletries	Gillette Avon	L'Oreal Nivea	Colgate Lancome
3341	Computer and peripheral equipment	HP Dell	Apple	Canon
3342	Communications equipment manufacturing	Nokia	Cisco	Blackberry
3343	Audio and video equipment manufacturing	Samsung Panasonic	Sony	Philips
3345	Electronic instrument manufacturing	Siemens		
3361	Motor vehicle manufacturing	Toyota Honda Audi Ferrari	Mercedes Ford Hyundai	BMW Volkswagen Porsche
3399	Other miscellaneous manufacturing	Nintendo	Cartier	
4481	Clothing stores	Zara	Gap	
4541	Electronic shopping and mail-order houses	Amazon.com	EBay	
5111	Newspaper, book, and directory publishers	Thomson Reuters		
5112	Software publishers	Microsoft Adobe	Oracle	SAP
5151	Radio and television broadcasting	Disney	MTV	
5191	Other information services	Google	Yahoo	
5221	Depository credit intermediation	J.P. Morgan	Santander	
5239	Other financial investment activities	Citi	UBS	
5241	Insurance carriers	AXA	Allianz	Zurich
5416	Management and technical consulting	Accenture		

Source: ESA calculations using Interbrand's Top 100 Global Brands and data from OneSource.

Trademark Registrations by Class

As discussed earlier, the USPTO organizes trademark registrations by class as opposed to industry. For several reasons, it is not possible to use the registration class data to identify trademark-intensive industries by four-digit NAICS industry. First, the classes are not sufficiently detailed for our purposes. There are 49 trademark classes, as opposed to 313 four-digit NAICS industries. So, even if it were possible to clearly define the correspondence between class and NAICS, a meaningful level of detail would be lacking.

Second, there is no straightforward correspondence between trademark classes and industries because the classes and NAICS industries are conceptually quite distinct. NAICS industries are defined according to the principal business activity of an establishment. Trademark classes indicate the type of good or service associated with a particular trademark. In a sense, the classes tell us what type of product is carrying the protected mark or logo. Consider the Whole Foods example cited earlier. Their "365 Everyday Value" logo appears on a wide range of goods covering 10 different trademark classes. As another example, consider Five Guys, the fast food franchise. This company has protected its "Five Guys" logo within six different trademark classes, ranging from meats and processed foods (for the sandwiches), to staple foods (processed peanut and fried potatoes), non-alcoholic beverages, advertising and business (franchising), clothing, and vehicles (to protect license plate holders with the logo).[57] Within the NAICS framework, however, Five Guys would simply be considered a limited-service eating place (NAICS 7222), a service-providing industry. So, while Five Guys is a service-provider under NAICS, most of its trademark classes relate to goods, that is, the "vessels" on which the company logo appears.

Despite the difficulty in precisely relating trademark classes to NAICS industries, it is worthwhile to look for similarities between the distribution of trademark registrations by class and our selection of trademark-intensive industries. Table 8 lists total registrations by trademark class for the period from November 16, 1999 to November 15, 2009, ranking the registration classes by trademark count. These data provide insight into which areas of the economy (by class) take advantage most often of trademark protection through the Federal trademark registration system.

The top seven categories accounted for more than half of all registrations in the 2000s. Three of these categories—advertising and business, education and entertainment, and insurance and financials—are very broad and cover services ranging from wholesale and retail trade to professional and business services; financial services; insurance; educational services; and the arts, entertainment, and recreation industry. At a superficial level, it rings true that these sectors rely on trademarks because they cover many of the services and brands that consumers use on a daily basis. Not surprisingly, several of the trademark-intensive industries correspond to these classes; however, many other industries do as well. On the other hand, consider the trademark classes for light beverages as well as wine and spirits, both of which would be expected to

---

[57] This trademark is serial number 85255019 and can be found by using the online search engine at *tarr.uspto.gov/servlet/tarr?regser=serial&entry=85255019.*

correspond to beverage manufacturing (NAICS 3121). This industry is clearly trademark-intensive as it was the only industry to be selected by all three criteria (trademark intensities, top 50 list, and sample). Furthermore, several beverages appeared in the top 100 brands Yet, the light beverages class only accounted for 0.8 percent of registrations (15,253) while wine and spirits accounted for 1.1 percent (20,727) for FY 2000 to FY 2009.

Table 8. Trademark Registrations by Class, Ranked by Number of Registrations, FY 2000-09

Trademark class	Class title	Trademark registrations		
		Total	Percent of total	Cumulative percent
9	Electrical and scientific apparatus	209,639	11.6%	11.6%
35	Advertising and business	184,274	10.2%	21.9%
41	Education and entertainment	151,547	8.4%	30.3%
42	Computer and scientific	136,025	7.5%	37.8%
16	Paper goods and printed matter	97,739	5.4%	43.2%
36	Insurance and financial	92,759	5.1%	48.4%
25	Clothing	91,923	5.1%	53.5%
5	Pharmaceuticals	57,081	3.2%	56.6%
28	Toys and sporting goods	53,292	3.0%	59.6%
3	Cosmetics and cleaning preparations	51,940	2.9%	62.5%
30	Staple foods	43,550	2.4%	64.9%
37	Building construction and repair	39,557	2.2%	67.1%
7	Machinery	36,683	2.0%	69.1%
38	Telecommunications	32,482	1.8%	70.9%
11	Environmental control apparatus	31,374	1.7%	72.7%
10	Medical apparatus	30,872	1.7%	74.4%
20	Furniture and articles, nec.	29,527	1.6%	76.0%
29	Meats and processed foods	27,188	1.5%	77.5%
1	Chemicals	27,009	1.5%	79.0%
44	Medical, beauty, and agricultural	26,404	1.5%	80.5%
12	Vehicles	25,891	1.4%	81.9%
43	Hotels and restaurants	25,825	1.4%	83.4%
39	Transportation and storage	25,562	1.4%	84.8%
21	Housewares and glass	25,356	1.4%	86.2%
6	Metal goods	21,724	1.2%	87.4%
14	Jewelry	21,422	1.2%	88.6%

Table 8. Trademark Registrations by Class, Ranked by Number of Registrations, FY 2000-09—Continued

Trademark class	Class title	Trademark registrations		
		Total	Percent of total	Cumulative percent
18	Leather goods	20,843	1.2%	89.7%
33	Wine and spirits	20,727	1.1%	90.9%
40	Treatment of materials	19,532	1.1%	92.0%
19	Nonmetallic building materials	17,801	1.0%	93.0%
32	Light beverages	15,253	0.8%	93.8%
31	Natural agricultural products	14,744	0.8%	94.6%
45	Personal	14,390	0.8%	95.4%
24	Fabrics	13,233	0.7%	96.2%
17	Rubber goods	11,637	0.6%	96.8%
8	Hand tools	11,098	0.6%	97.4%
2	Paints	8,352	0.5%	97.9%
4	Lubricants and fuels	7,502	0.4%	98.3%
34	Smokers' articles	5,004	0.3%	98.6%
27	Floor coverings	4,771	0.3%	98.8%
26	Fancy goods	4,698	0.3%	99.1%
22	Cordage and fibers	3,809	0.2%	99.3%
13	Firearms	3,628	0.2%	99.5%
15	Musical instruments	3,555	0.2%	99.7%
200	Collective membership	1,577	0.1%	99.8%
23	Yarns and threads	1,423	0.1%	99.9%
B	Services certification mark	1,391	0.1%	100.0%
A	Goods certification mark	765	0.0%	100.0%
	Total	**1,802,378**	**100.0%**	**100.0%**

Source: ESA calculations using unpublished USPTO data.

Note: The cumulative percent figures may not equal the sum of the percent of total figures because of rounding.

Copyrights

Overview

Copyrights, the third form of IP rights covered in this report, protect "original works of authorship."[58] These works must be fixed in a tangible form of expression, meaning that concepts that never leave the confines of our minds cannot be copyrighted. Protection under copyright, which lasts for the life of the author plus an additional 70 years, is secured automatically when a work is created.[59] Neither publication nor registration with the Copyright Office is required to secure copyright protection. But registering a copyright does establish a public record of the copyright, and it can be beneficial because of incentives provided to encourage registration. For example, a registered copyright can be recorded with the U.S. Customs and Border Protection to protect against the importation of infringing copies.[60]

More than 33.7 million copyrights have been registered in the United States since 1790, when Congress enacted the first Federal copyright law. Of these, approximately 150,000 were registered between 1790 and the centralization of copyright functions in the Library of Congress in 1870.[61] In 2009, more than 382,000 basic copyrights were registered.

The types of works that can be copyrighted are outlined in the 1976 Copyright Act. A partial list of copyrighted materials includes the following:

- literary works (including fiction, nonfiction, and computer programs)

- musical works, including any accompanying words

- dramatic works, including any accompanying music

- pantomimes and choreographic works

- pictorial, graphic, and sculptural works

- motion pictures and other audiovisual works

- sound recordings

- architectural works, including vessel hull designs

Of the 382,000 registrations in 2009, about 93,000 covered performing arts works, such as films, musical and dramatic works, and choreography. There were 75,000 registrations of works

---

[58] U.S. Copyright Office 2008, 2.

[59] A work is "created" when it is fixed in a copy for the first time, regardless of whether the work is published or not.

[60] U.S. Copyright Office 2008, 7.

[61] See the Brief History of the Copyright Office at *www.copyright.gov/circs/circ1a.html*. Copyright registration data are published in U.S. Copyright Office 2009, 68.

of visual and applied arts. These covered fine and graphic arts, sculptures, technical drawings and models, photographs and cartographic works, and commercial prints and labels. Registrations of sound recordings totaled 42,000.[62]

Identifying Copyright-Intensive Industries

Our methodology for designating copyright-intensive industries draws heavily from definitions established by the World Intellectual Property Organization's (WIPO) *Guide on Surveying the Economic Contribution of the Copyright-based Industries.*[63] A series of reports by Stephen Siwek entitled *Copyright Industries in the U.S. Economy* have applied these definitions to the U.S. economy.[64] While this established literature underlies our analysis, we used a more narrow definition of copyright-intensive industries than WIPO, focusing on industries that produce copyrighted work and excluding several industries associated with the distribution of copyrighted material. This deviation from the WIPO Guide was needed in order to maintain internal consistency with our measures of patent- and trademark-intensive industries.

Methodology

Because WIPO's *Guide on Surveying the Economic Contribution of the Copyright-based Industries* clearly distinguishes the type of works that can be copyrighted, the industries in which those works are created, and the downstream (distribution) industries delivering the produced copyrighted works, it is possible to develop a list of copyright-intensive industries that is comparable in scope to our lists of patent- and trademark-intensive industries. We started by focusing on "core" copyright industries, which WIPO defines as industries "wholly engaged in creation, production and manufacturing, performance, broadcast, communication and exhibition, or distribution and sales of works and other protected subject matter."[65] In other words, core copyright industries are considered 'core' because they either produce copyrighted materials or bring them to market.

For this report, we are only concerned with the set of industries that are primarily responsible for the *creation or production* of copyrighted materials and designate them as copyright-intensive. Thus, to the extent possible using four-digit NAICS industry codes, we excluded industries whose primary purpose is to distribute copyright materials to businesses, consumers, or both. For example, we did not count industries such as book, periodical, and music stores (NAICS 4512) or consumer goods rental (NAICS 5322), which includes video rentals, as copyright-intensive even though they are part of the "core" category in the WIPO guide.[66] Our

---

[62] Ibid., 69.

[63] World Intellectual Property Organization 2003.

[64] See, for example, Siwek 2009.

[65] World Intellectual Property Organization 2003, 29. The core copyright industries represent one of four main groups of copyright-based industries. The others are interdependent, partial, and non-dedicated support industries.

[66] This discussion should not imply that distribution industries as a whole cannot by our definitions be considered IP-intensive. As discussed above, a broad range of industries seek trademark protection, including distribution industries like clothing stores, which are identified as IP-intensive.

definition is narrower than WIPO's in order to be consistent with our treatment of patent- and trademark-intensive industries, where the industries most responsible for the production of protected IP are the main focus. This approach simply reflects our goal of examining the industries in the economy that are most responsible for the production of protected IP and use of this approach is not a criticism of WIPO's guidelines.

One conceptual distinction between the approach taken here and that selected in the patent and trademark sections is worth noting. Throughout this report, the focus was on industries that produce protected IP, whether patents, trademarks, or copyrights. In the case of patents and trademarks, we defined "intensive" industries as the subset of all patent or trademark producers that had high scores in various "intensity" measures, whereas we defined as copyright-intensive essentially all industries associated with the production of copyrighted materials.

Results

Table 9 lists the copyright-intensive industries. All are involved in the creation and/or recording (in print, magnetically, or digitally) of protected works. For industries such as other information services (NAICS 5191), the title of which does not clearly indicate what protected materials are produced, the relevant copyrighted product is listed in parentheses.

Table 9. Copyright-Intensive Industries

NAICS code	Industry title
5111	Newspaper, periodical, book, and directory publishers
5112	Software publishers
5121	Motion picture and video industries
5122	Sound recording industries
5151	Radio and television broadcasting
5152	Cable and other subscription programming
5191	Other information services (news syndicates and internet sites)
5414	Specialized design services (visual and graphic arts)
5415	Computer systems design and related services (software and databases)
5418	Advertising, public relations, and related services
5419	Other professional, scientific, and technical services (photography and translation)
7111	Performing arts companies
7115	Independent artists, writers, and performers

Source: ESA selection based on World Intellectual Property Organization 2003.

Some of the selected industries are involved in both the production and distribution of copyrighted materials since both functions are often performed within a single business establishment.[67] The newspaper industry provides a good example of the blurry line between the creation and distribution of copyrighted materials. We considered newspaper, periodical, book and directory publishers (NAICS 5111) to be copyright-intensive because much copyrighted material actually is developed within establishments classified in this industry, as evidenced by the fact that this industry had 31,000 reporters and correspondents, 25,000 graphic designers, and 4,000 photographers on its payrolls in 2010.[68]

This line of reasoning underlies the inclusion of several industries on the list, such as sound recording, broadcasting, cable programming, and performing arts companies. These industries have many "creators" (writers, composers, choreographers, and others) directly on their payrolls, in addition to other independent artists and content creators under individual contracts with their companies.

Our list of copyright-intensive industries also includes two additional industries directly involved in the writing and publishing of newspapers: independent artists, writers, and performers (NAICS 7115) and other information services (NAICS 5191), which includes news syndicates. However, we excluded printing and related support activities (NAICS 3231), because its role is simply to print the newspapers themselves. WIPO considers this a "core" copyright industry because it is directly involved in creating a "vessel" for copyrighted material, meaning that it exists in order to deliver copyrighted materials in a tangible form to a consumer or audience. However, printing is distinct from the actual development of the copyrighted materials (such as news articles and photographs), so we did not consider it to be a copyright-intensive industry.

As another example, consider the manufacturing and reproducing magnetic and optical media industry (NAICS 3346). This industry produces software CDs and DVDs, as well as other prerecorded disks, tapes and vinyl records. While inextricably linked to copyright-intensive industries, this industry is not part of the actual process of developing and recording software or music, but rather a part of the downstream process of putting the material on a tangible vessel. So as with the printing example above, while manufacturing and reproducing magnetic and optical media is a WIPO-defined core industry, it is not counted as copyright-intensive in this report. It should be noted, however, that both printing and related support activities (NAICS 3231) and manufacturing and reproducing magnetic and optical media (NAICS 3346) were found to be trademark-intensive.

---

[67] World Intellectual Property Organization 2003, 27.

[68] These data are from the Bureau of Labor Statistics, Occupational Employment Statistics program and are for private wage and salary workers in newspaper, periodical, book and directory publishers (NAICS 5111). See *www.bls.gov/oes/current/naics4_511100.htm#27-0000.*

IP-Intensity and the Use of Intellectual Property Protection

Before reviewing the complete list of IP-intensive industries, we should note that defining "IP intensity" as the use of intellectual property protection is an approach open to criticism. Although commonly used in the scientific literature, such intensity measures tend to overweight those industries that more commonly use patents, trademarks, or copyrights for purposes other than activities closely related to R&D or commercialization *per se*.[69]

The term "IP-intensive" defined in this report is not necessarily directly related to the value or purpose of the IP held by companies. In some industries a single patent may support revenues in the billions of dollars, while in other industries, many patents may be required just to market marginally profitable products.[70, 71] The same logic holds for trademarks and copyrights.[72]

For example, the Carnegie-Mellon University survey, previously mentioned, shows significant differences across industries in how companies acquire and use patents.[73] These findings are not surprising. First, companies employ other protections, such as trade secrets, that may be a substitute for patent protection. And, because the term of protection is limited, patent efficacy can be diminished by lengthy product and process development. Often companies will seek patent protection early in that timeline (as patent costs remain relatively inexpensive in the United States), only to determine after further research and development that the patent protection was neither needed nor particularly useful in the final outcome.

Prior economic studies have also shown that patents can be used for defensive purposes, and our method for selecting IP-intensive industries necessarily sweeps widely, including industries in which companies seek patent protection regardless of the purpose.[74] To understand the various motivations for patenting, the Carnegie-Mellon study also focused on the reasons companies in different industries sought patent protection and the multiple uses of patents. The reasons included earning licensing revenue, use in negotiations, blocking competitors, enhancing reputation, or as a measure of employee performance. The research found that companies reported that their patents often served multiple purposes. All drug companies surveyed, for instance, used product patenting to prevent copying, while 97 percent used product patenting to block competitors, 69 percent to enhance the company's reputation, and 61 percent to aid in

---

[69] Jaffe and Trajtenberg 2002.

[70] The pharmaceutical industry is a prime example of the former. Merck & Company, for instance, lost billions of dollars in sales beginning in 2008 on the osteoporosis drug Fosamax when generic manufacturers successfully invalidated its core patent. See Higgins and Graham 2009, 370-71.

[71] Electronics products are prime examples of the latter, as products from Motorola, Samsung, and Nokia, now competing with Apple's iPhone in the hand-held market, all require the rights to many patents in order to be legally sold in the U.S. market.

[72] The appendix to this report examines the extent to which industries selected as IP-intensive have relatively high revenue shares from the licensing of rights to use protected intellectual property and other IP-related product lines.

[73] Cohen et al. 2000.

[74] Hall and Ziedonis 2001.

negotiations.   In the aerospace industry, 57 percent of companies reported using product patents for licensing revenue, while 50 percent of those companies used process patents for the same purpose. Among companies in the machine tool sector, 13 percent reported that they used product patents as a measure of employees' performance. Collectively, these findings show that the term "use" is complex at the company level, and that complexity must be acknowledged in interpreting the aggregated measures we report at the industry level.

IP-Intensive Industries

Seventy-five IP-intensive industries emerged after combing through the lists of patent-, trademark-, and copyright-intensive industries. (See Table 10.) This 75-industry total is smaller than the sum of the parts. Indeed, there is considerable overlap between the patent-intensive and trademark-intensive industry lists, as 18 of the 26 patent-intensive industries also were identified among the 60 trademark-intensive ones. There also is some overlap between the copyright-intensive and trademark-intensive list with six of the 13 copyright-intensive industries also selected as trademark-intensive. By definition, however, there is no overlap between the patent and copyright lists. The USPTO classified all patents within manufacturing industries, whereas industries involved in the creation and/or recording of protected works are classified as service-providing industries and not in the manufacturing sector.

Table 10 also lists total employment of each IP-intensive industry. Employment refers to wage and salary jobs as well as self-employment, which accounts for a sizeable portion of employment in the copyright-intensive industries.[75] Employment in IP-intensive industries totaled 27.1 million jobs in 2010. The next section will examine in more detail their contribution to overall employment and gross domestic product in the U.S. economy as well as workers' wages, educational attainment, and foreign trade.

---

[75] Unpaid family workers also are included in the employment estimates from the BLS Industry Productivity program. However, because unpaid family workers account for only about one percent of the combined total of the self-employed and unpaid family workers outside of agriculture, they are not referred to or analyzed elsewhere in this report.

Table 10. IP-Intensive Industries and Selection Criteria

NAICS code	Industry title	Employment in 2010 (1000 jobs)	Patent-intensive	Trademark-intensive	Copyright-intensive
			Selection criteria		
2111	Oil and gas extraction	163.3		X	
2361	Residential building construction	934.3		X	
3112	Grain and oilseed milling	58.3		X	
3113	Sugar and confectionery product manufacturing	69.9		X	
3115	Dairy product manufacturing	130.4		X	
3119	Other food manufacturing	165.5		X	
3121	Beverage manufacturing	169.5		X	
3162	Footwear manufacturing	13.5		X	
3221	Pulp, paper, and paperboard mills	112.7		X	
3222	Converted paper product manufacturing	285.9		X	
3231	Printing and related support activities	524.4		X	
3251	Basic chemical manufacturing	143.1	X	X	
3252	Resin, rubber, and artificial fibers	90.1	X	X	
3253	Agricultural chemical manufacturing	36.7	X		
3254	Pharmaceutical and medicine manufacturing	277.6	X	X	
3255	Paint, coating, and adhesive manufacturing	56.4	X		
3256	Soap, cleaning compound, and toiletries	104.2	X	X	
3259	Other chemical product and preparations	84.9	X	X	
3261	Plastics product manufacturing	501.5		X	
3322	Cutlery and handtool manufacturing	42.1		X	
3329	Other fabricated metal product manufacturing	256.4		X	
3331	Ag., construction, and mining machinery manufacturing	208.9	X		
3332	Industrial machinery manufacturing	102.2	X	X	
3333	Commercial and service industry manufacturing	91.3	X	X	
3334	HVAC and commercial refrigeration	124.4	X		
3335	Metalworking machinery manufacturing	156.1	X		
3336	Turbine and power transmission equipment manufacturing	91.5	X	X	
3339	Other general purpose machinery manufacturing	229.8	X	X	
3341	Computer and peripheral equipment	161.9	X	X	
3342	Communications equipment manufacturing	118.5	X	X	
3343	Audio and video equipment manufacturing	20.2	X	X	

Table 10. IP-Intensive Industries and Selection Criteria—Continued

NAICS code	Industry title	Selection criteria			
		Employment in 2010 (1000 jobs)	Patent-intensive	Trademark-intensive	Copyright-intensive
3344	Semiconductor and electronic component manufacturing	373.8	X		
3345	Electronic instrument manufacturing	408.7	X	X	
3346	Magnetic media manufacturing and reproducing	26.3	X		
3351	Electric lighting equipment manufacturing	46.2	X		
3352	Household appliance manufacturing	60.7	X	X	
3353	Electrical equipment manufacturing	137.3	X	X	
3359	Other electrical equipment and components	118.7	X	X	
3361	Motor vehicle manufacturing	151.8		X	
3371	Household and institutional furniture	245.8		X	
3391	Medical equipment and supplies manufacturing	311.5	X	X	
3399	Other miscellaneous manufacturing	309.6	X	X	
4234	Commercial equip merchant wholesalers	615.4		X	
4242	Druggists' goods merchant wholesalers	193.3		X	
4244	Grocery and related product wholesalers	735.3		X	
4451	Grocery stores	2,521.6		X	
4481	Clothing stores	1,114.4		X	
4511	Sporting goods and musical instrument stores	514.6		X	
4541	Electronic shopping and mail-order houses	303.9		X	
5111	Newspaper, book, and directory pub	530.9		X	X
5112	Software publishers	259.8		X	X
5121	Motion picture and video industries	414.6		X	X
5122	Sound recording industries	36.4			X
5151	Radio and television broadcasting	216.7		X	X
5152	Cable and other subscription programming	85.6		X	X
5174	Satellite telecommunications	14.6		X	
5179	Other telecommunications	127.5		X	
5191	Other information services	145.5		X	X
5221	Depository credit intermediation	1,735.6		X	
5239	Other financial investment activities	427.4		X	
5241	Insurance carriers	1,368.2		X	
5311	Lessors of real estate	823.9		X	
5331	Lessors of nonfinancial intangible	25.5		X	

Table 10. IP-Intensive Industries and Selection Criteria—Continued

NAICS code	Industry title	Employment in 2010 (1000 jobs)	Selection criteria		
			Patent-intensive	Trademark-intensive	Copyright-intensive
5414	Specialized design services	242.6			X
5415	Computer systems design and related services	1,595.1			X
5416	Management and technical consulting	1,233.8		X	
5417	Scientific research and development	638.2		X	
5418	Advertising, PR, and related services	461.2			X
5419	Other professional and technical services	673.4			X
5614	Business support services	883.9		X	
5615	Travel arrangement and reservation	201.7		X	
6214	Outpatient care centers	636.6		X	
7111	Performing arts companies	132.1			X
7115	Independent artists, writers, and performers	306.1			X
7132	Gambling industries	133.9		X	

Source: ESA calculations using data from the Bureau of Labor Statistics' Industry Productivity program.

Note: Employment includes wage and salary jobs, the self-employed, and unpaid family workers and is measured in thousands of jobs.

III. IP-INTENSIVE INDUSTRIES IN THE ECONOMY

Employment

Employment totaled 27.1 million jobs in IP-intensive industries in 2010, representing 18.8 percent of all jobs in the economy. (See Figure 1.) Our definition of jobs includes not just payroll (or wage and salary workers), but also the self-employed and unpaid family workers.[76] Labor market analyses of this type often overlook the self-employed, but as will be seen, they are a critical source of staff for copyright-intensive industries, and to a lesser extent, for trademark-intensive industries.

Figure 1. Employment in IP-Intensive Industries, 2010

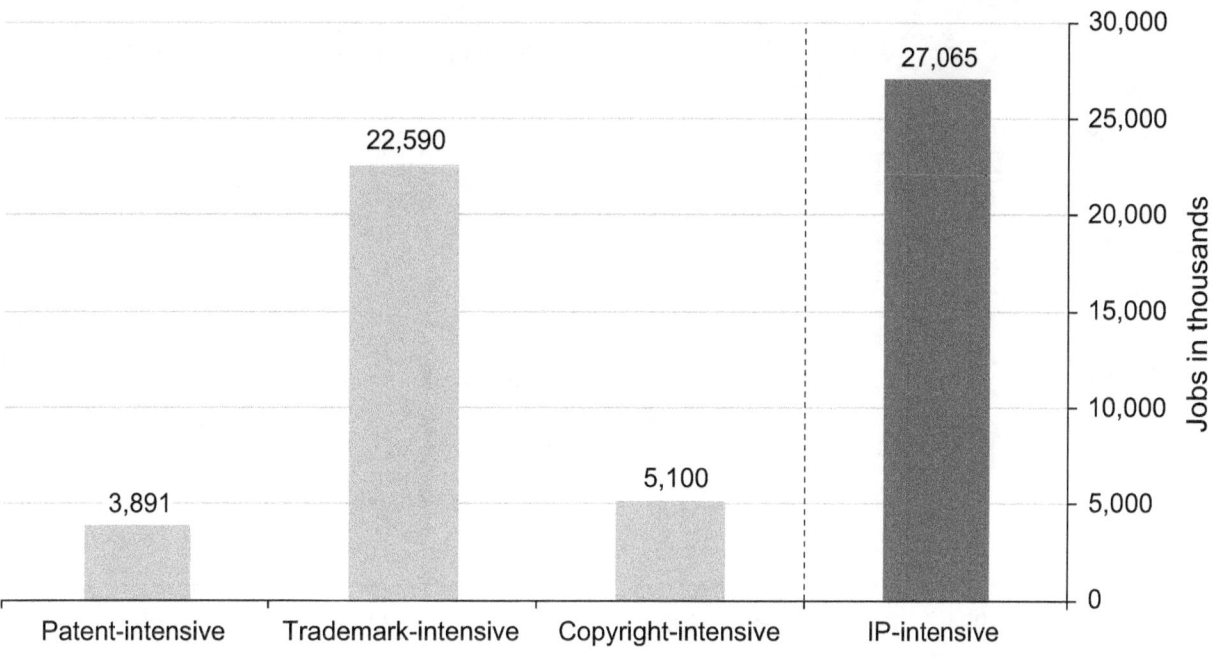

Source: ESA calculations using data from the Bureau of Labor Statistics' Industry Productivity program.

Note: Estimates include wage and salary employment, the self-employed, and unpaid family workers. Because several industries were found to be trademark-intensive and patent- or copyright-intensive, total employment in IP-intensive industries is less than the sum of employment in patent-, trademark-, and copyright-intensive industries.

Given that 60 of the 75 IP-intensive industries were considered trademark-intensive, it follows that these industries would account for the majority of IP-intensive jobs (22.6 million or 83 percent of all IP-intensive jobs). Indeed, employment in the patent- and copyright-

---

[76] As noted earlier, the employment data cited here were provided by the Bureau of Labor Statistics' Industry Productivity program. Employment covers the sum of payroll jobs, self-employed persons, and unpaid family workers and totaled 144.2 million jobs in 2010. Because the unit of measure is jobs (as opposed to persons) and because about 5 percent of all workers have more than one job, the total number of jobs is greater than the 139.1 million employed persons in 2010, as estimated from the Current Population Survey (*www.bls.gov/cps*).

intensive industries was significantly lower. In 2010, patent-intensive industries had 3.9 million jobs and copyright-intensive industries had 5.1 million jobs. The 24 industries that were considered intensive with respect to more than one form of IP protection had 4.5 million jobs.[77]

As can be seen in Figure 2, employment growth over the past two decades has varied considerably across IP-intensive industries. The figure compares the relative job growth in the various industry groupings since 1990. Employment in IP-intensive industries in 2010 was little changed from 1990 as the 12-percent growth in employment during the 1990s was subsequently reversed during the 2000s. In contrast, non-IP-intensive employment grew in the 1990s and had relatively flat employment in the 2000s.[78] As a result, the IP-intensive industries' share of total employment edged down from 21.7 percent in 1990 to 20.7 percent in 2000 and declined nearly 2 more percentage points by 2010 to 18.8 percent.

Figure 2. Indexed Employment in IP-Intensive Industries, 1990-2011

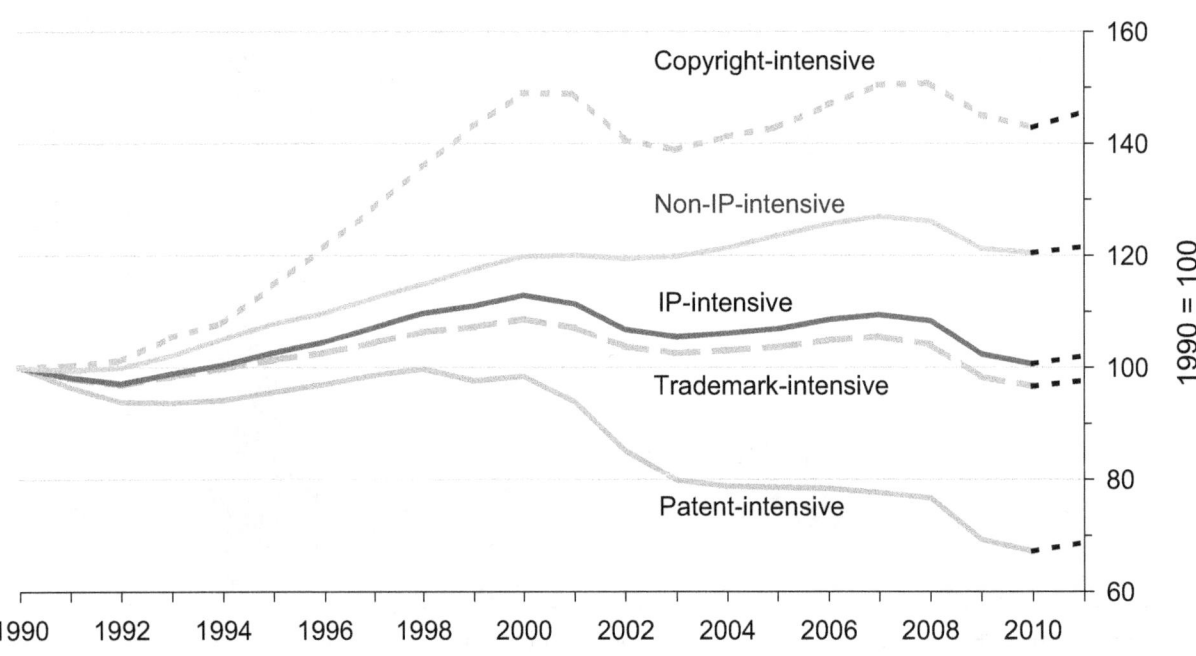

Source: ESA calculations using data from the Bureau of Labor Statistics' Industry Productivity program.

Note: Black dotted lines represent ESA projections of 2011 employment growth based on data from the Bureau of Labor Statistics' Current Employment Statistics program.

Overall employment in IP-intensive industries has lagged other industries over the past two decades due primarily to historic losses in manufacturing jobs. This decline tracks with other statistics showing that during the last decade the economy was underinvesting and underperforming in manufacturing. For much of the 2000s, manufacturing capacity remained stagnant, and for the first time in decades, manufacturing firms' real investment in fixed assets

---

[77] The 4.5 million jobs figure can be calculated by subtracting overall IP-intensive employment from the sum of employment of the trademark-, patent-, and copyright-intensive industries.

[78] Non-IP-intensive employment refers to employment in private sector industries not selected as IP-intensive, plus employment in government and in private households.

stagnated.[79] During this same period, the U.S. manufacturing sector lost more than 3 million jobs.[80]

Over the two decades, shrinking employment in patent-intensive industries was offset by expansion in the copyright-intensive ones. Patent-intensive industries are a subset of the manufacturing sector, and its job losses are much like those experienced throughout the nation's manufacturing sector. The copyright-intensive industries largely belong to the information and professional and technical services industry sectors in NAICS, and their employment trends parallel the trends seen in those sectors: steady growth in the 1990s and offsetting gains and losses in the 2000s.[81] That is, job growth between 2000 and 2010 in professional and technical services was largely offset by employment declines in the information industries.

As the economic recovery has unfolded, real business fixed investment in equipment and software has rebounded, growing by nearly 33 percent from the second quarter of 2009 through the end of 2011.[82] At the same time, manufacturing production surged at a 5.7 percent annual rate from June 2009 through December 2011, the fastest pace of growth of production in a decade.[83] The resurgence in production led manufacturers to add 346,000 factory jobs in 2010 and 2011, the strongest two-year period of manufacturing job growth since the late 1990s.[84]

Preliminary employment projections from the Economics and Statistics Administration for 2011 show that as the economic recovery has taken hold, IP-intensive industry employment has rebounded and contributed disproportionately to overall employment growth. As shown in Figure 2, job growth was widespread, with a 1.6 percent rise in employment in IP-intensive industries outpacing the 1.0 percent increase in non-IP-intensive industries. Breaking IP-intensive industries out into its constituent parts uncovers 2.4 percent job growth in copyright-intensive industries, 2.3 percent growth in patent-intensive industries, and 1.1 percent growth in trademark-intensive industries.

---

[79] Data on industrial capacity published by the Federal Reserve Board and data on private fixed investment by industry from the Bureau of Economic Analysis' Fixed Assets Accounts Table 3.8ES, as cited in White House 2012, 1 and 7. The data are available at *www.federalreserve.gov/releases/g17/caputl.htm* and *www.bea.gov/iTable/index_FA.cfm*.

[80] Data from the Bureau of Labor Statistics' Current Employment Statistics program, available at *www.bls.gov/ces*.

[81] The copyright-intensive industries from the information sector are newspaper, periodical, book and directory publishers; software publishers; motion picture and video industries; sound recording industries; radio and television broadcasting; cable and other subscription programming; and other information services. The copyright-intensive industries drawn from the professional and technical services sector are specialized design services; computer systems design and related services; advertising, public relations, and related services; and other professional, scientific, and technical services.

[82] See Bureau of Economic Analysis' National Income and Product Accounts, Table 1.1.6, available online at *http://www.bea.gov/iTable/index_nipa.cfm*.

[83] Data on industrial production are published by the Federal Reserve Board, with historical data available at *www.federalreserve.gov/releases/g17/table1_2.htm*.

[84] Data from the Bureau of Labor Statistics' Current Employment Statistics program, available at *www.bls.gov/ces*.

In 2010, the self-employed filled 2.4 million jobs in IP-intensive industries. This 8.9 percent self-employment share was essentially equal to the 8.8 percent share in other (non-IP-intensive) industries; however, there was notable variation across IP-intensive industries (See Figure 3). Trademark-intensive industries had the largest number of self-employed persons at 1.7 million or 7.3 percent of all trademark-intensive jobs. The highest self-employment share, however, was in the copyright-intensive industries, in which the 0.8 million self-employed workers filled 16.5 percent of all jobs. This high share is not surprising as many jobs in the creative and performing arts are contract rather than payroll jobs, usually related to the completion or performance of a specific authored work.

Figure 3. Self-Employed Share of All Jobs in IP-Intensive Industries, 2010

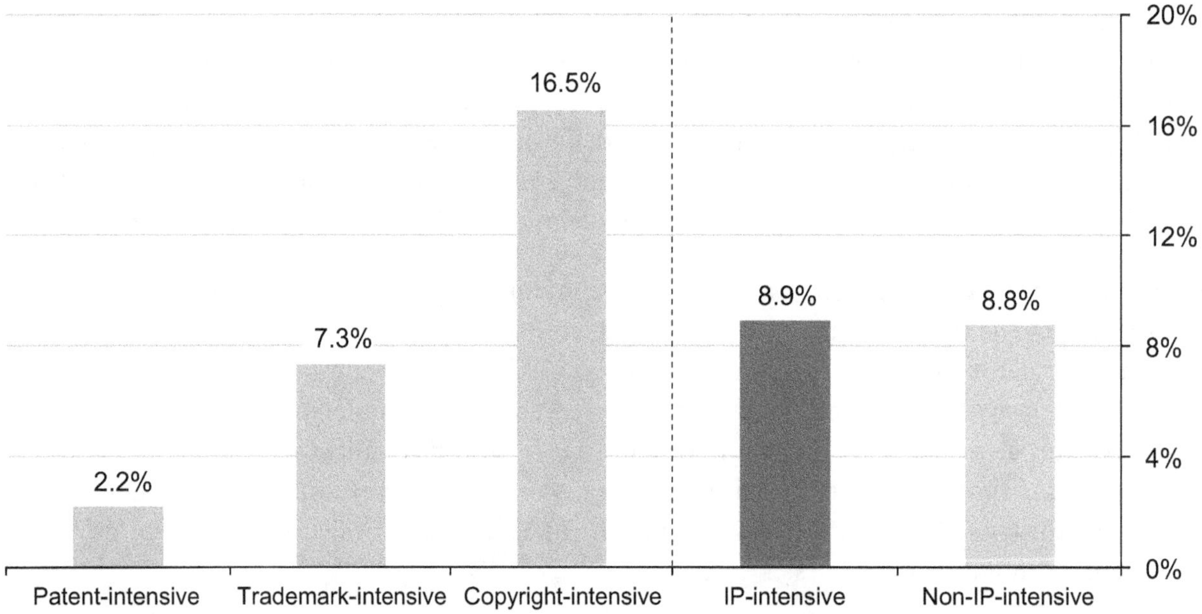

Source: ESA calculations using data from the Bureau of Labor Statistics' Industry Productivity program.

Note: Estimates show the self-employed and unpaid family workers as a share of all jobs. However, unpaid family workers account for only about one percent of the combined total of the self-employed and unpaid family workers outside of agriculture.

Total Employment Supported by IP-Intensive Industries

While IP-intensive industries had 27.1 million jobs either on their payrolls or under contract in 2010, these industries indirectly supported an additional 12.9 million jobs in other (non-IP-intensive) industries throughout the economy. In other words, IP-intensive industries supported 40.0 million jobs (or 27.7 percent of all jobs) directly and indirectly, through a supply chain that stretches across the economy.[85]

Figure 4 expands on Figure 1, showing employment in IP-intensive industries (medium blue bar) plus indirect employment in the supply chain (the rectangle below the blue bar). The figure also shows the jobs that the patent-, trademark-, and copyright-intensive industries support in their respective (non-patent-, trademark-, and copyright-intensive) supply chains. Thus, as shown, patent-intensive industries supported an additional 3.3 million workers indirectly. Likewise, trademark-intensive industries supported 13.1 million jobs indirectly, and copyright-intensive industries indirectly via the supply chain supported 2.5 million jobs.

Figure 4. Total Employment Supported by IP-Intensive Industries, 2010

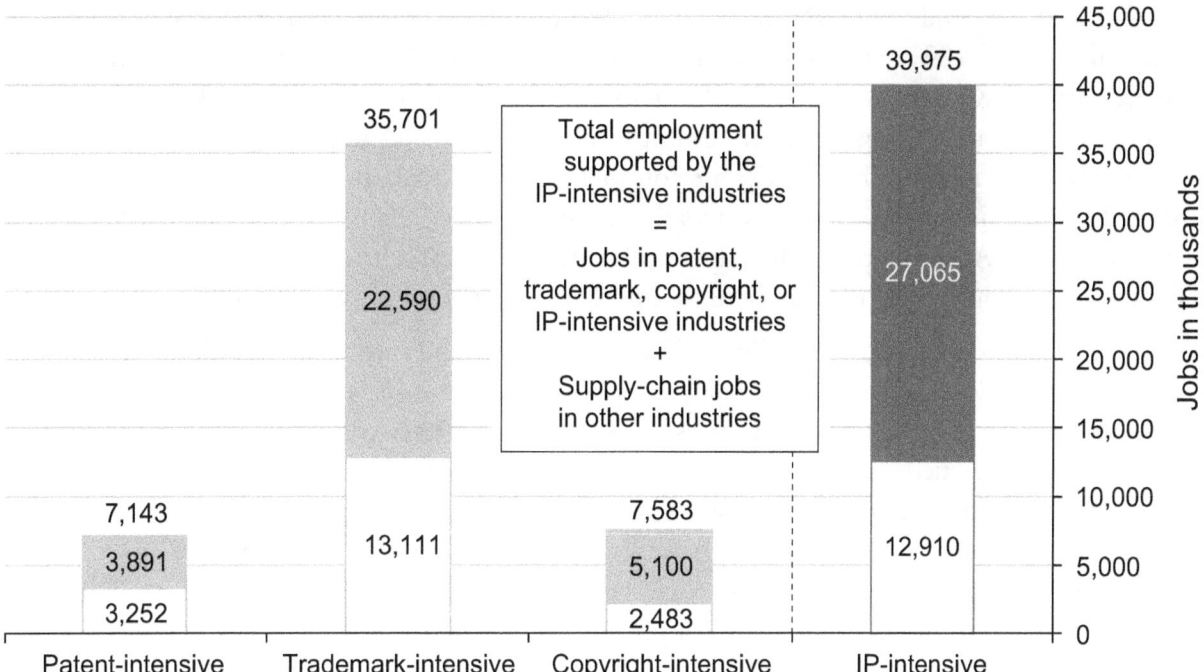

Source: ESA calculations using data from the Bureau of Economic Analysis' Industry Accounts office and the Bureau of Labor Statistics' Industry Productivity program.

Note: Estimates include wage and salary employment, the self-employed, and unpaid family workers.

---

[85] These estimates are derived from unpublished input/output tables computed and analyzed by staff from the Bureau of Economic Analysis' Industry Accounts office. Data are consistent with the December 2010 annual revision to the annual input/output tables and are based on the 2009 after-redefinition domestic make and use tables and estimates of the share of 2010 employment attributable to final demand in IP-intensive industries. Total output requirement tables were calculated based on the make and use table following the methodology published in mathIO.doc, which are available at *www.bea.gov/industry/zip/cxctr2002detail.zip.*

As these data suggest, patent-intensive industries relied more deeply than the trademark- and copyright-intensive industries on an outside supply chain and indirectly supported a relatively large number of jobs. Consider that the patent-intensive industries, despite being smaller in terms of employment than the copyright-intensive ones, supported a larger multiple of outside supply chain employment. This is because patent-intensive industries come from the manufacturing sector, which typically has a larger multiplier effect than the service sector, from which the copyright-intensive industries are drawn.

Additionally, as the "intensive" industry lists become longer, the number of "non-intensive" industries, which is the source of the indirect, supply chain jobs, becomes shorter. This is why trademark-intensive industries alone indirectly supported 13.1 million workers, while IP-intensive industries as a whole indirectly supported only 12.9 million workers. This is also why the 60 trademark-intensive industries were more likely to self-supply some of their inputs than the 26 patent-intensive industries and less likely to rely on outside industries. Put another way, the potential outside supply chain (indirect jobs) for patent-intensive industries was larger (covers more industries) than the potential supply chain for the trademark-intensive industries.

These results may appear conservative relative to multiplier analyses often cited in the economic literature with employment multipliers of about 2. Such multipliers tell us that if growing demand for final goods and services (as opposed to intermediate inputs to production) spurs companies to add 100 new jobs, then an additional 100 jobs will be added indirectly throughout the economy.[86] We estimated that for IP-intensive industries this multiplier would be about 1.8, which is close to the multiplier of 2 found in similar industry analyses. As noted earlier, because a relatively large number of industries are considered IP-intensive, much of the IP supply chain is internal to these industries, which reduces the multiplier effect relative to analyses that focus on a single industry. At the extreme, the jobs-to-jobs multiplier could be calculated for the entire economy and would be 1 because there would be no external supply chain left.

In this report, the question that is being addressed differs subtly from the question that can be answered by a traditional multiplier analysis. Rather than focusing on a hypothetical change in final demand for IP-intensive goods and services, we were interested in learning which IP-intensive jobs were tied to final demand, which were in the supply chain, and how many jobs in other industries were part of that supply chain. Teasing out these data from the input/output framework, we estimated that 16.2 million jobs in IP-intensive industries were associated with producing goods and services to satisfy final demand while 10.9 million jobs in these industries were associated with production for the supply chain. An additional 12.9 jobs in other (non-IP-intensive industries) also were part of the IP supply chain.[87]

---

[86] In Miller and Blair 1985, these multipliers are referred to as "type I employment multipliers," while in the Bureau of Economic Analysis 1997, they are referred to as direct-effect employment multipliers.

[87] The 16.2 million jobs in IP-intensive industries directly linked to final demand was found by examining the share of IP output associated with final demand (excluding imports). We then fed the vector of final demand IP-intensive employment into a jobs-to-jobs total requirements matrix in several iterations until we accounted for all 27.1 million jobs in the IP-intensive industries. The first iteration told us that a total of 29.4 million jobs were associated with the 16.2 million final-demand, IP-intensive jobs, giving us the 1.8 multiplier figure we cite. This first iteration, however, only accounted for about 20 million jobs in IP-intensive industries. Subsequent iterations uncovered the full set of supply chain jobs in IP-intensive industries as well as the full supply chain in other (non-IP-intensive) industries.

As is typical with input/output analyses, these data emphasize upstream industries (supply chain) that provide intermediate inputs needed to produce goods and services in IP-intensive industries. They do not, however, capture the significant downstream channels that facilitate the distribution and trade in IP-intensive goods and services. Therefore, the estimate that there were 40.0 million jobs supported by IP-intensive industries is actually a conservative estimate of employment linked to these industries.

Value Added

While IP-intensive industries accounted for 18.8 percent of all jobs in the economy in 2010, their $5.06 trillion in value added in 2010 represented 34.8 percent of total GDP.[88] This total share of GDP has edged down since 2003. Because 60 of the 75 IP-intensive industries were considered trademark-intensive, it is unsurprising that this segment alone accounted for almost 31 percent of GDP with $4.5 trillion in value added in 2010. (See Figure 5.) Patent-intensive and copyright-intensive industries accounted for 5.3 and 4.4 percent of GDP, with $763 billion and $641 billion in value added, respectively.

Figure 5. Value Added and Employment Shares of IP-Intensive Industries, 2010

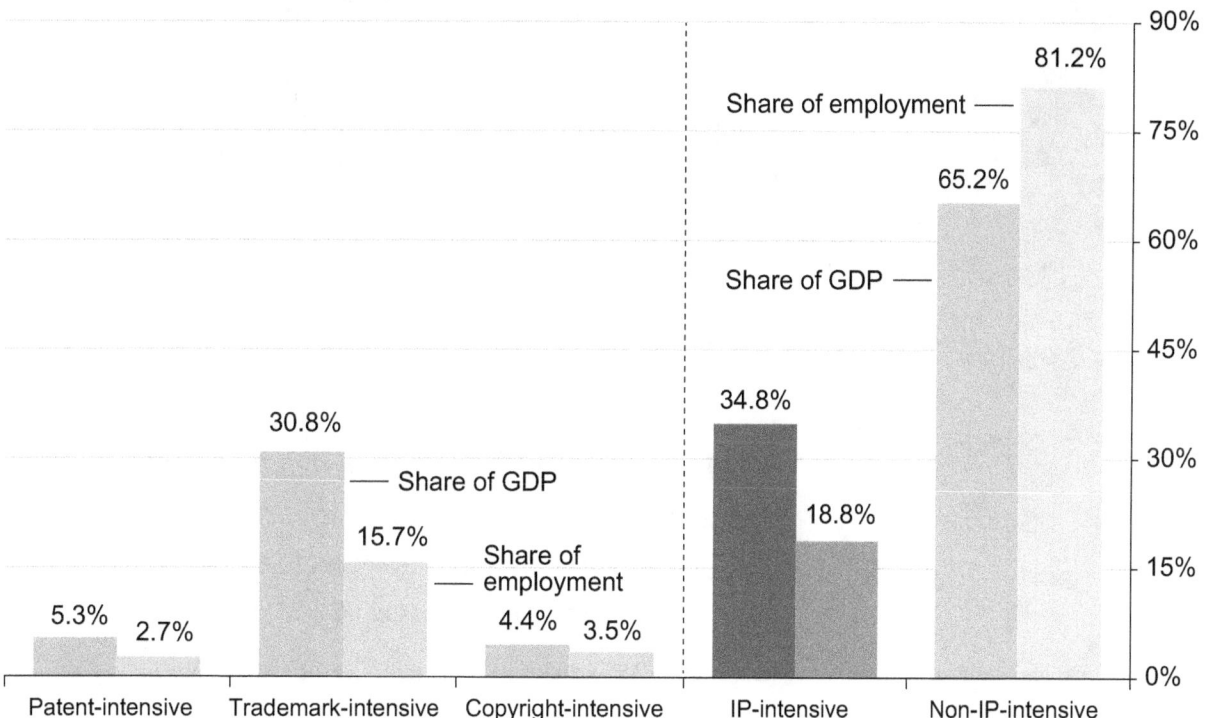

Source: ESA calculations using data from the Bureau of Economic Analysis, National Income and Product Accounts and the Bureau of Labor Statistics' Industry Productivity program.

---

[88] Value added is defined as the difference between an industry's total output (its sales plus the change in inventories arising from production) and the value of its intermediate purchases from other industries (that is, from its supply chain). GDP can be defined as the sum of value added across all industries in the economy. When value added is summed across all industries, industry sales to and purchases from each other cancel out, and the remainder is industry sales to final users, or GDP.

Payroll Employment by State in IP-Intensive Industries

The IP-intensive share of all covered employment varies notably across states and regions, as shown in Map 1.[89] Four of the top five states in IP-intensive employment share were in New England: Massachusetts (23.6 percent), New Hampshire (22.0 percent), Connecticut (21.7 percent), and Vermont (21.6 percent). Wisconsin, with a 23.0 percent share, occupied second place on the list. Overall there were 16 states above the national average of 19.1 percent. These states were spread throughout the mid-Atlantic, Northeast, and Midwest and also include California, Colorado, and Utah.

Map 1. IP-Intensive Industries' Share of Covered Employment by State, 2010

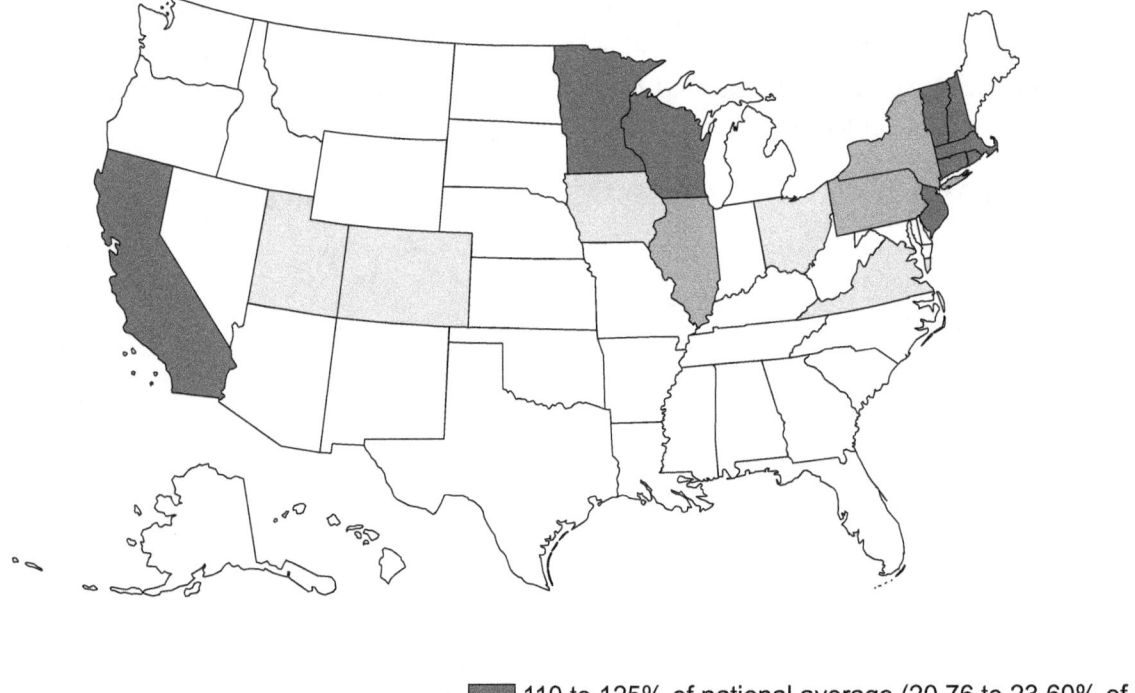

■ 110 to 125% of national average (20.76 to 23.60% of jobs)

■ 105 to 109% of national average (20.00 to 20.75% of jobs)

□ 100 to 105% of national average (19.05% to 19.99% of jobs)

□ Below national average (<19.05% of jobs)

Source: ESA calculations using data from the Bureau of Labor Statistics' Quarterly Census of Employment and Wages.

---

[89] The data used to examine state employment are from the Bureau of Labor Statistics' Quarterly Census of Employment and Wages (QCEW) and measure covered employment. Covered employment refers to jobs covered by state and Federal unemployment insurance law, and includes practically all civilian wage and salary employment. These data do not include the self-employed or unpaid family workers. For more information on QCEW, see *www.bls.gov/cew*.

Given that 60 of the 75 IP-intensive industries were designated as trademark-intensive, it is not surprising to find that 15 of the 16 states with above-average shares of IP-intensive jobs also had above-average shares of trademark-intensive jobs. (See Map 2.) Only Virginia had a high percentage of IP-intensive jobs, but a below-average share of trademark-intensive employment, as 14.2 percent of employment in the state was in trademark-intensive industries, below the national average of 16.2 percent.

Map 2. Trademark-Intensive Industries' Share of Covered Employment by State, 2010

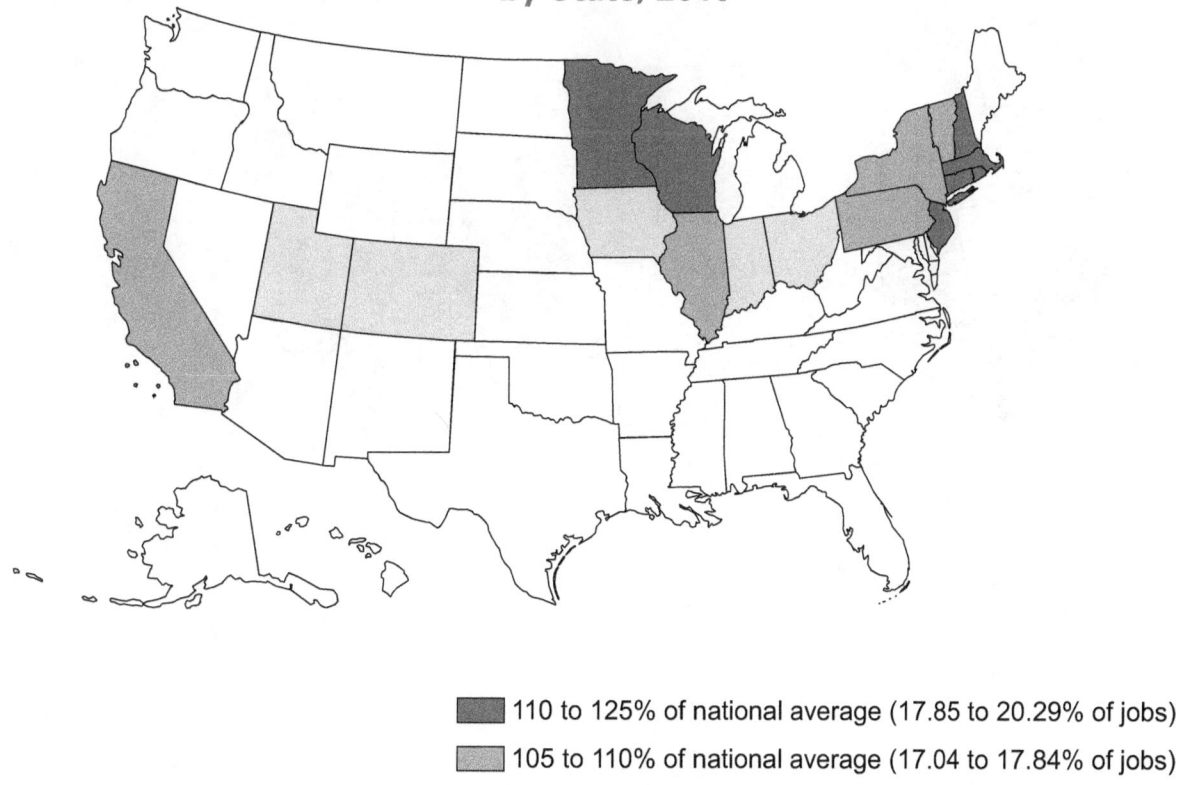

- 110 to 125% of national average (17.85 to 20.29% of jobs)
- 105 to 110% of national average (17.04 to 17.84% of jobs)
- 100 to 105% of national average (16.23% to 17.03% of jobs)
- Below national average (<16.23% of jobs)

Source: ESA calculations using data from the Bureau of Labor Statistics' Quarterly Census of Employment and Wages.

As highlighted in Map 3, there were 21 states with patent-intensive employment shares above the 3.0 percent national average. States from New England and the Midwest had the highest shares, led by New Hampshire (5.2 percent), Wisconsin (4.9 percent), and Minnesota, Indiana, and Vermont (4.4 percent each). Essentially all regions of the country had at least one state with an above-average percentage of employment in patent-intensive industries, including the South with North Carolina, South Carolina, and Tennessee.

Map 3. Patent-Intensive Industries' Share of Covered Employment by State, 2010

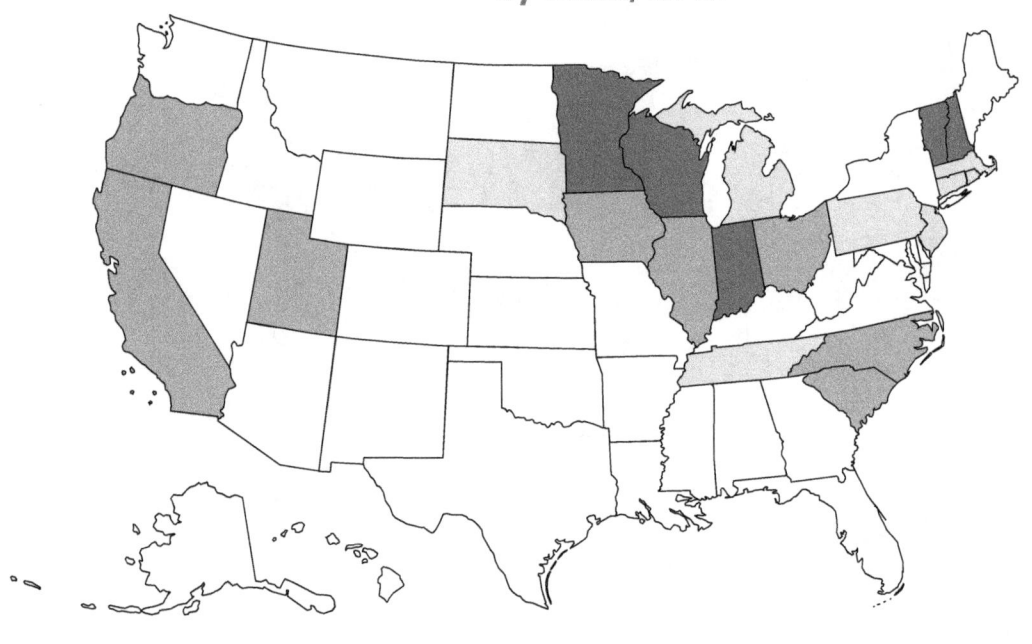

■ 150 to 176% of national average (4.38 to 5.20% of jobs)

■ 120 to 150% of national average (3.50 to 4.37% of jobs)

□ 100 to 120% of national average (2.92 to 3.49% of jobs)

□ Below national average (<2.92% of jobs)

Source: ESA calculations using data from the Bureau of Labor Statistics' Quarterly Census of Employment and Wages.

The 13 states with above-average employment shares in copyright-intensive industries were mostly spread along the East and West coasts, as seen in Map 4. The District of Columbia (6.4 percent), Virginia (5.9 percent), and New York (4.9 percent) had copyright-intensive employment shares more than 1.5 times above the national average of 3.3 percent. They were followed by Washington State, California, and Colorado (4.7 percent each). Utah and Minnesota were the only other non-coastal states on the list.

Map 4. Copyright-Intensive Industries' Share of Covered Employment by State, 2010

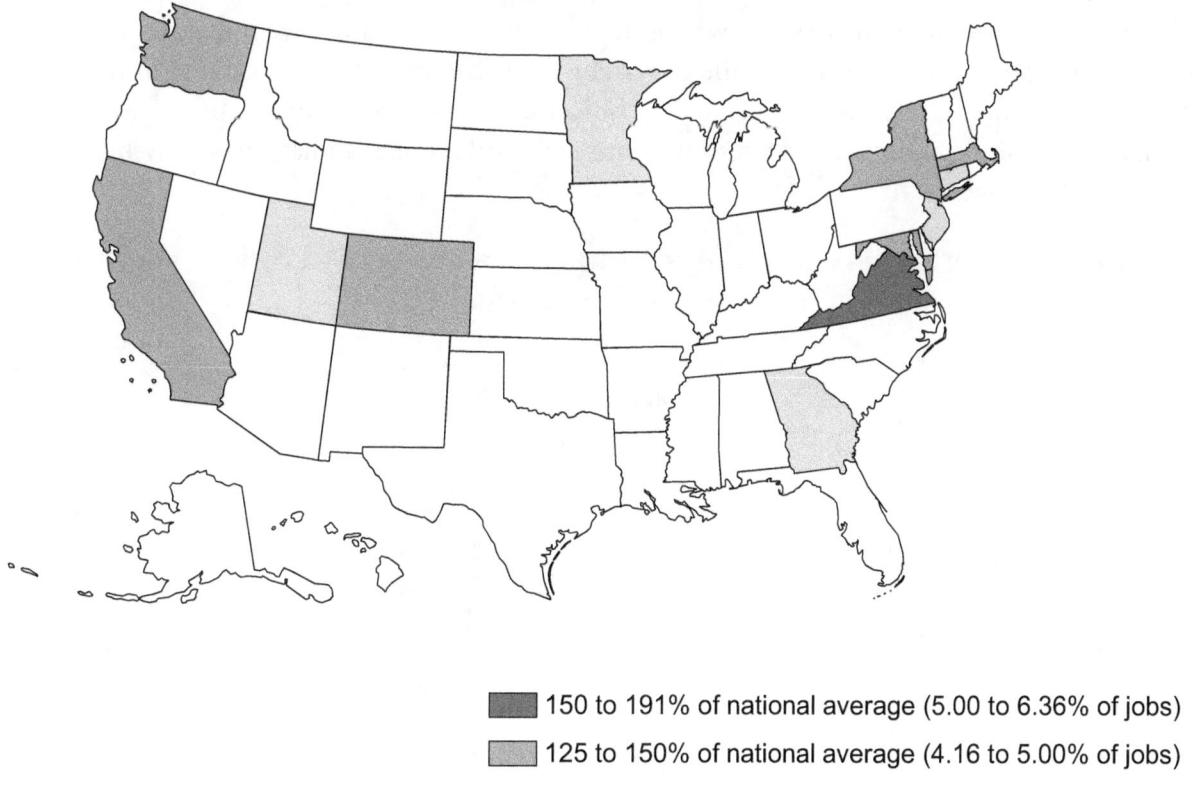

■ 150 to 191% of national average (5.00 to 6.36% of jobs)

■ 125 to 150% of national average (4.16 to 5.00% of jobs)

□ 100 to 125% of national average (3.33% to 4.16% of jobs)

□ Below national average (<3.33% of jobs)

Source: ESA calculations using data from the Bureau of Labor Statistics' Quarterly Census of Employment and Wages.

Putting these rankings together, we found six states that had above-average employment shares for patent-, trademark-, and copyright-intensive industries: California, Connecticut, Massachusetts, Minnesota, New Jersey, and Utah. These results echo an underlying theme of this report—intellectual property permeates our entire economy. Industries from a broad range of economic sectors are IP-intensive, and the jobs they support span all regions of the United States.

Average Weekly Wages

Private wage and salary workers in IP-intensive industries had average weekly wages of $1,156 in 2010, or 42 percent higher than workers in non-IP-intensive industries in the private sector.[90] (See Figure 6.) This difference was even higher for workers in patent-intensive industries, who earned $1,407 per week on average, and in copyright-intensive industries, with weekly wages of $1,440. Workers in trademark-intensive industries earned $1,111 per week, less than their counterparts in patent-intensive and copyright-intensive industries. This may reflect the fact that trademark-intensive industries represent a wider range of industries than patent-intensive and copyright-intensive industries. As was outlined earlier, patent-intensive industries are a subset of manufacturing industries, while copyright-intensive ones are concentrated in the information sector and the professional and technical services sector. Workers in manufacturing, information, and professional and technical services all have relatively high average weekly wages.

Figure 6. Average Weekly Wages of Private Wage and Salary Workers in IP-Intensive Industries, 2010

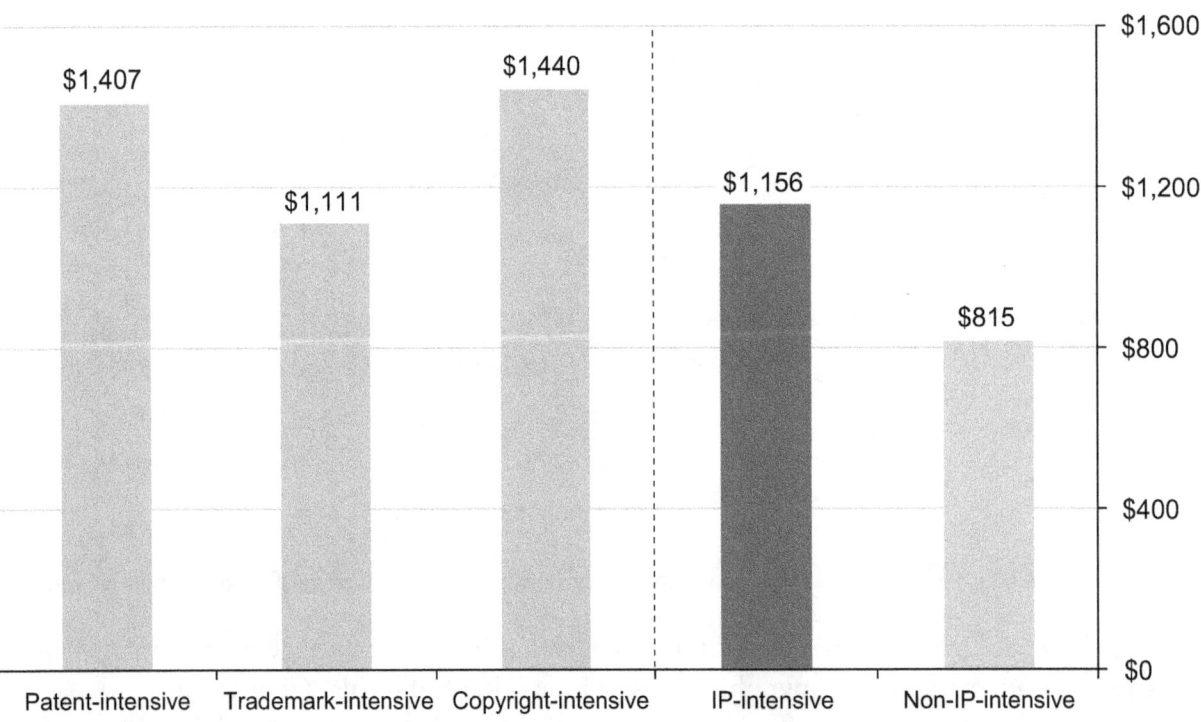

Source: ESA calculations using data from the Bureau of Labor Statistics' Quarterly Census of Employment and Wages.

---

[90] This section focuses on the average weekly earnings of private wage and salary workers using data from the QCEW. According to QCEW data, there were 24.5 million private wage and salary jobs in IP-intensive industries in 2010. Wages represent total compensation paid during the calendar year, regardless of when services were performed. Included in wages are pay for vacation and other paid leave, bonuses, stock options, tips, the cash value of meals and lodging, and in some states, contributions to deferred compensation plans (such as 401(k) plans).

The premium for working in an IP-intensive industry has grown over time, as shown in Figure 7. In 1990, IP-intensive jobs paid 22 percent more than jobs in other industries and a decade later this premium had risen to 38 percent. It lost some ground early in the 2000s before edging back up and reaching a new high of 42 percent in 2010. Trademark-intensive industries followed a similar but slightly lower upward path over the past two decades. In 1990, trademark-intensive industries paid 20 percent more on average than non-IP-intensive industries, with this premium climbing to 31 percent by 2000 and 36 percent in 2010. Wages in patent-intensive industries started out at a 46 percent premium in 1990, and this premium grew through the 1990s before surging up to 69 percent by 2000. This surge was reversed in 2001, and the premium changed little in the last decade before rising again over the past few years. In 2010, patent-intensive workers earned 73 percent more per hour than workers in non-IP industries.

Copyright-intensive industries followed a more extreme version of the trends outlined above. Workers in these industries earned 30 percent more than non-IP workers on average in 1990, and this premium tripled during the following decade to 88 percent in 1999. Over the next five years, the premium decreased to 64 percent before growing again to 77 percent in 2010.

Figure 7. Average Weekly Wage Premium of Workers in IP-Intensive Industries Relative to Non-IP-Intensive Industries, 1990-2010

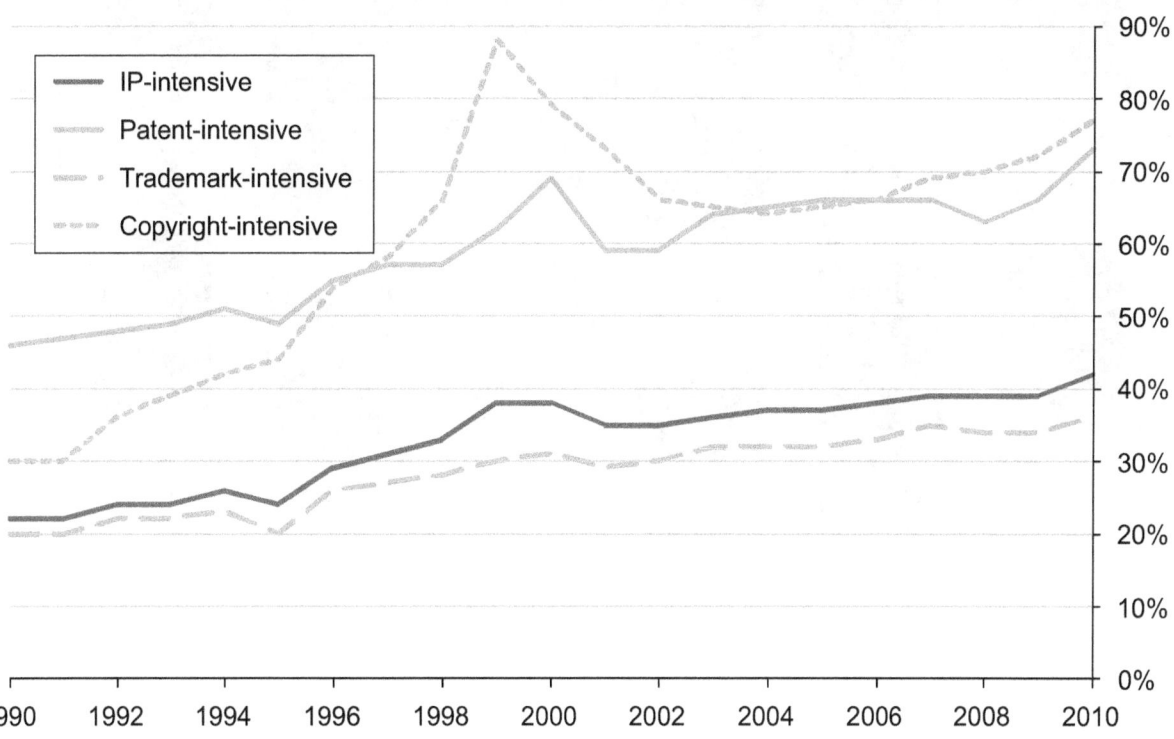

Source: ESA calculations using data from the Bureau of Labor Statistics' Quarterly Census of Employment and Wages.

Educational Attainment

In competitive labor markets, wages are closely correlated to worker productivity, and educational attainment is a common gauge of workers' skills and expected productivity. Thus, it would be expected that employees in IP-intensive industries have relatively high educational attainment. The data bear that out as 42.4 percent of workers age 25 and older in the IP-intensive industries in 2010 had a bachelor's degree or higher, compared with 34.2 percent in private non-IP-intensive industries.[91] (See Figure 8.) Workers in copyright-intensive industries were the most educated of the three IP-intensive segments with 61.2 percent having attained a bachelor's degree or higher, and only 1.7 percent having less than a high school diploma. Essentially identical shares of workers in the patent- and trademark-intensive industries (38.7 and 38.8 percent, respectively) had at least a bachelor's degree.

Figure 8. Distribution of Employed Persons in IP-Intensive Industries by Educational Attainment, 2010

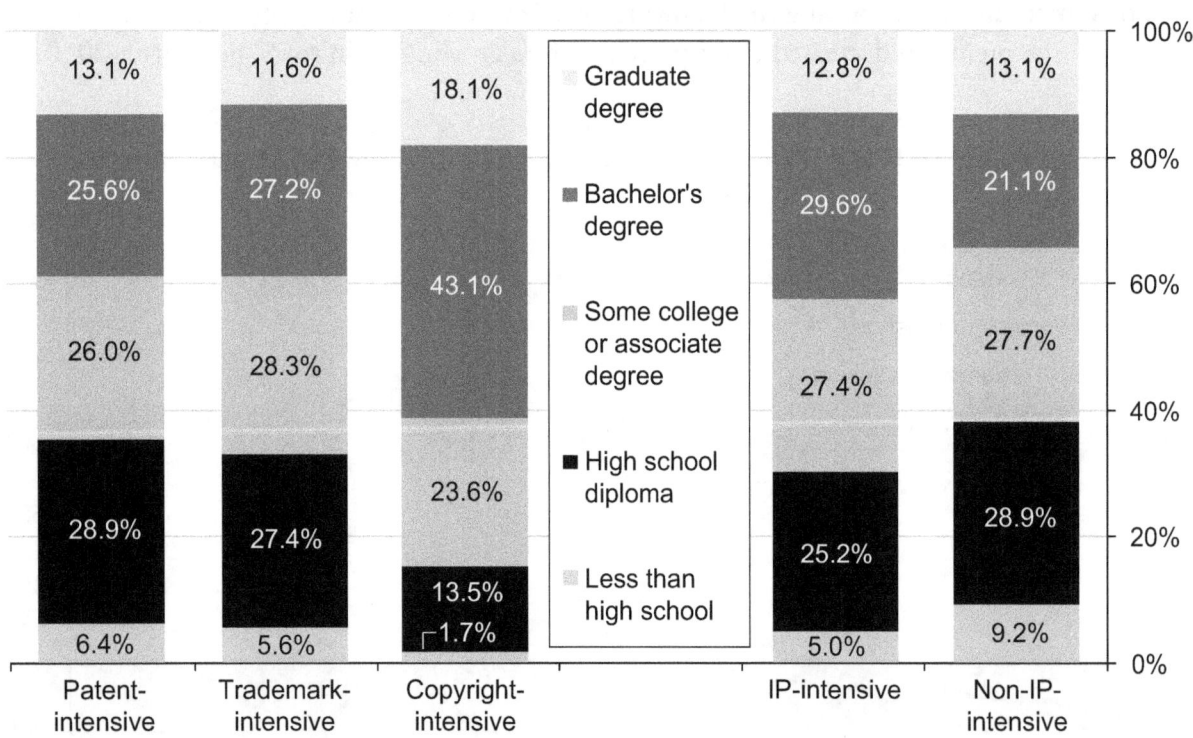

Source: ESA calculations using Current Population Survey public-use microdata.

Note: Estimates are for employed persons age 25 and over.

---

[91] These estimates are calculated from 2010 Current Population Survey public-use microdata, as accessed through the Census Bureau's DataFerrett tool at *dataferrett.census.gov*.

Foreign Trade

Although trade statistics do not tell us anything about the IP content of exports or imports, U.S. IP-intensive industries are a major part of U.S. trade. Merchandise exports of IP-intensive industries totaled $775 billion in 2010, accounting for 60.7 percent of total U.S. merchandise exports, while merchandise imports of IP-intensive industries stood at $1,336 billion or 69.9 percent of total U.S. merchandise imports. From 2000 to 2010, exports of IP-intensive industries increased 52.6 percent while imports of IP-intensive industries rose 61.6 percent.

Manufacturing industries were responsible for almost 99 percent of IP-intensive merchandise exports in 2010, with oil and gas extraction and software publishing accounting for the rest. Exports from the semiconductors and electronic parts sector led the way, totaling $64.0 billion or 8.3 percent of IP-intensive industries' merchandise exports. (See Figure 9.) The next largest export categories were basic chemicals ($58.4 billion), motor vehicles ($52.4 billion), pharmaceuticals and medicine ($49.4 billion), and computer and peripherals ($44.1 billion).

Figure 9. Merchandise Exports of Selected IP-Intensive Industries, 2010

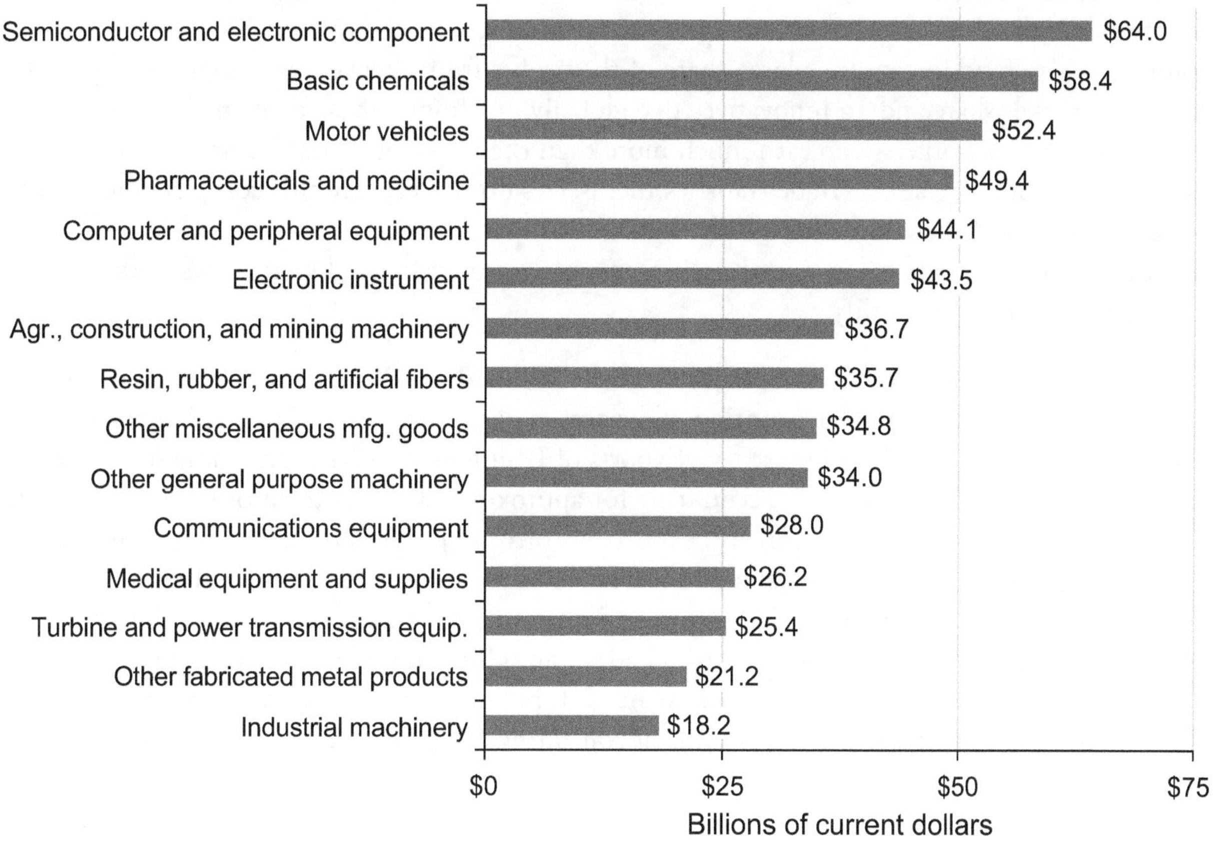

Source: ESA calculations using data from the Census Bureau's Foreign Trade Division.
Note: The selected industries accounted for 74 percent of merchandise exports of IP-intensive industries.

On the imports side, manufacturing accounted for 79 percent of total imports of IP-intensive industries while oil and gas represented 21 percent and software publishing less than 1 percent. Among imports of manufactured goods, the largest category was motor vehicles (9.7 percent of all imports of IP-intensive industries), followed by computers and peripheral equipment (6.7 percent) and pharmaceuticals and medicines (6.5 percent).

It should be noted that the imports of goods of IP-intensive industries included those produced by U.S.-owned establishments located overseas and by foreign producers under U.S. licenses. In 2009, Americans received $89.8 billion from royalties and license fees, which included industrial processes and trademarks, while paying foreigners $25.2 billion. Imports also provide benefits for American consumers and industries. Imports tend to increase market competition and thus lower prices, making some products affordable to more American consumers. Likewise, many imports are intermediate inputs for American industries which make their finished products more competitive.[92]

More generally, one must keep in mind that trade statistics do not convey the importance of IP-intensive products to the U.S. economy. For instance, U.S. electronics companies like Apple tend to capture a significant portion of the value added in their global supply chain from products like the iPod and iPhone, two products that are assembled offshore.[93] These companies also tend to capture a large share of the profits from their global supply chains while retaining market share and an innovative edge globally. At home, these companies employ many high-skilled workers who earn much more than the low-wage, low-skill workers that assemble products overseas.[94] Trade statistics themselves do not capture this complete picture of the contribution of these industries to the U.S. economy and its competitiveness. A casual examination of the trade balance in the IP-intensive electronics-related sectors misses this nuanced and important reality.

Data on foreign trade of services are more limited. We used the 2007 Economic Census in order to get the most detailed accounting of services exports and to calculate total exports of IP-intensive service-providing industries. Exports of IP-intensive service-providing industries totaled about $90 billion in 2007, accounting for approximately 19 percent of total U.S. private services exports. As shown in Figure 10, exports of software publishers, at $22.3 billion, were the largest group of services exports in 2007, followed by the motion picture and video industry at $15.3 billion. Other major services export categories in 2007 included financial investment activities ($12.3 billion, excluding securities and commodity contracts intermediation and brokerage), scientific research and development ($10 billion), depository credit intermediation ($6.9 billion), and management and technical consulting ($6.3 billion).

---

[92] An estimated 53 percent of U.S. merchandise imports were intermediate products in 2007, according to unpublished data from Koopman et al. 2010.

[93] Linden, Dedrick, and Kraemer 2010.

[94] Linden, Dedrick, and Kraemer 2009.

Figure 10. Exports of IP-Intensive Service-Providing Industries, 2007

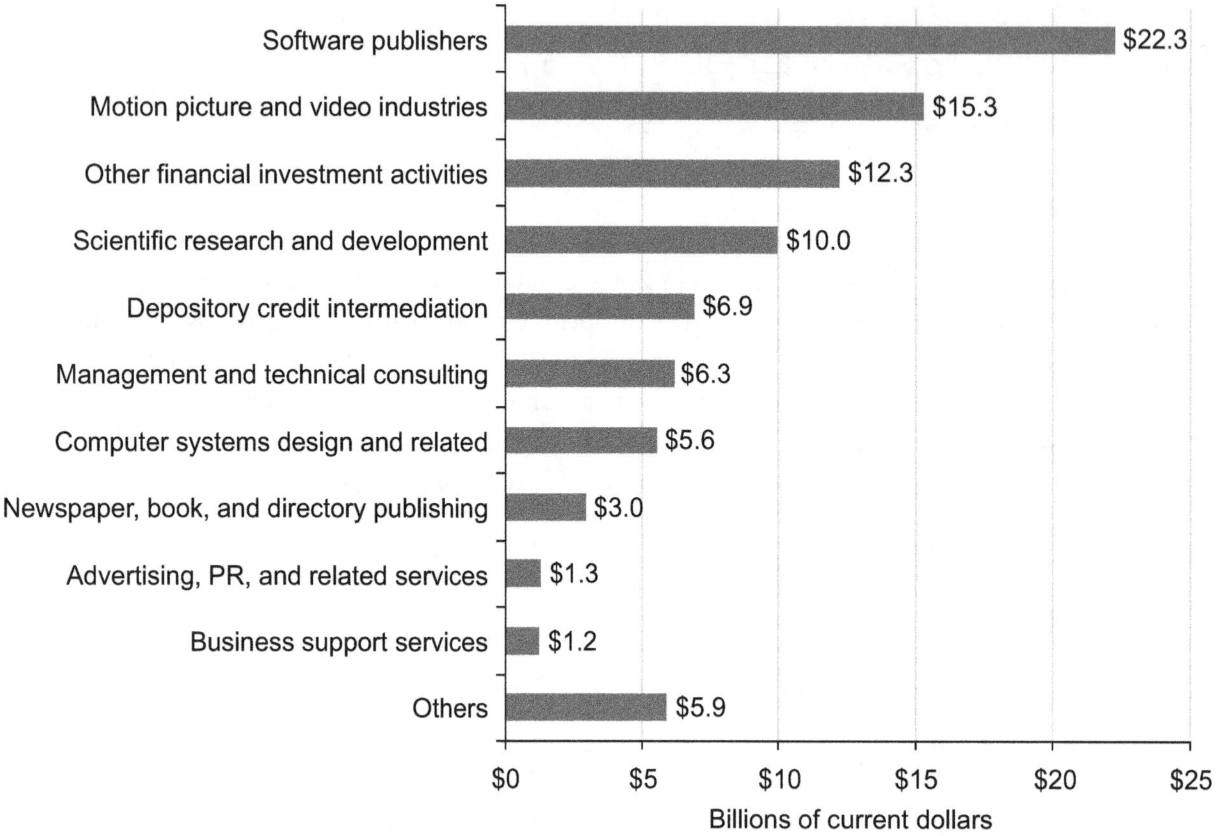

Industry	Billions
Software publishers	$22.3
Motion picture and video industries	$15.3
Other financial investment activities	$12.3
Scientific research and development	$10.0
Depository credit intermediation	$6.9
Management and technical consulting	$6.3
Computer systems design and related	$5.6
Newspaper, book, and directory publishing	$3.0
Advertising, PR, and related services	$1.3
Business support services	$1.2
Others	$5.9

Billions of current dollars

Source: ESA calculations using data from the Census Bureau's 2007 Economic Census.

Appendix

Revenue Generated from the Licensing of Rights to Use Protected Intellectual Property

Every five years, the Census Bureau conducts an Economic Census of U.S. business establishments, with the latest conducted in 2007. Data collected include number of employees, annual payroll, and value of sales by specific product lines. As a robustness measure of our list of IP-intensive industries, we examined the extent to which industries with high revenue share from IP-related product lines were among our 75 IP-intensive industries. Specifically, we identified 91 product codes from the Economic Census that were associated with licensing, royalties, and other forms of trade of intellectual property.

Examples of such product codes include:

- Licensing of rights:

  - to use intellectual property (product code 39400)

  - to use intellectual property-protected by copyright (39401)

  - to use intellectual property-protected as industrial property (39402)

  - to use intellectual property-protected by trademark (39403)

  - to use intellectual property-protected by patent (39404)

- Outright sale of:

  - original works of intellectual property (39250)

  - intellectual property protected by copyright (31500)

- "Contract production" of various forms of intellectual property (product codes 30150, 31510, 31520, 35113, 35111, 35114, 35115, 35112, 35110, 35540) and "exclusivity" rights (product code 31256)

Table 11 shows the 31 four-digit NAICS industries that had at least some IP-related revenue, ranked by the IP share of total revenue in 2007. The distribution of IP-related revenue was fairly concentrated. Ten industries had IP revenue shares above the 6.6 percent average (among industries with IP-related revenue), and these industries accounted for about 95 percent of total revenue from IP-related products. All but one of the ten industries also were identified in this

report as IP-intensive. The sole exception was promoters of performing arts, sports, and similar events (NAICS 7113). This industry generated 6.2 percent of its revenue in 2007 from a few IP-related areas, including exclusivity rights; licensing of rights to use property protected by trademark; licensing of rights to use property protected by copyright; contract production services for intellectual property protected by copyright, excluding live performing arts; and contract production services for intellectual property protected by trademark.[95]

Overall, 14 of the 31 industries with any revenue generated by the protection of IP products and services in 2007 made it into our IP-intensive industry list. Of the 17 industries that were not defined as IP-intensive, four were in the broader education sector and four were in the "other services (except public administration)" sector.

---

[95] See *factfinder.census.gov/servlet/IBQTable?_bm=y&-ds_name=EC077113&-NAICS2007=7113&-_lang=en.*

Table 11. Industries with IP-Related Revenue, Ranked by IP-Revenue Intensity, 2007

	NAICS code	IP-intensive	Industry title	IP-related revenue ($millions)	Cumulative share	IP-revenue intensity (IP/total revenue)
	7115	X	Independent artists, writers, and performers	$9,776	6.8%	76.6%
	5331	X	Lessors of nonfinancial intangible assets	24,473	23.7%	74.3%
	5121	X	Motion picture and video industries	51,132	59.2%	64.1%
	5152	X	Cable and other subscription programming	17,256	71.1%	38.4%
	5122	X	Sound recording industries	5,290	74.8%	34.8%
	7111	X	Performing arts companies	3,208	77.0%	23.6%
	5112	X	Software publishers	12,868	86.0%	9.5%
	5417	X	Scientific research and development services	8,532	91.9%	9.0%
	5191	X	Other information services	2,812	93.8%	7.5%
	7113		Promoters of performing arts, sports, and similar events	999	94.5%	6.2%
	7112		Spectator sports	1,024	95.2%	3.4%
	8139		Professional and similar organizations	1,822	96.5%	3.2%
	7114		Agents and managers for public figures	80	96.5%	1.6%
	5511		Management of companies and enterprises	1,349	97.5%	1.3%
	5151	X	Radio and television broadcasting	628	97.9%	1.1%
	6114		Business schools and computer and management training	107	98.0%	1.1%
	5111	X	Newspaper, periodical, book, and directory publishers	883	98.6%	0.6%
	5413		Architectural, engineering, and related services	1,130	99.4%	0.4%
	6117		Educational support services	37	99.4%	0.4%
	8132		Grantmaking and giving services	258	99.6%	0.3%
	8133		Social advocacy organizations	64	99.6%	0.3%
	5419	X	Other professional, scientific, and technical services	86	99.7%	0.2%
	5179	X	Other telecommunications	54	99.7%	0.2%
	8134		Civic and social organizations	23	99.7%	0.2%

Above mean +1 std. dev.

Above mean

Table 11. Industries with IP-Related Revenue, Ranked by IP-Revenue Intensity, 2007—Continued

NAICS code	IP-intensive	Industry title	IP-related revenue ($millions)	Cumulative share	IP-revenue intensity (IP/total revenue)
5415	X	Computer systems design and related services	287	99.9%	0.1%
7121		Museums, historical sites, and similar institutions	20	100.0%	0.1%
6116		Other schools and instruction	19	100.0%	0.1%
5171		Wired telecommunications carriers	19	100.0%	0.0%
5418	X	Advertising, public relations, and related services	16	100.0%	0.0%
5172		Wireless telecommunications carriers (except satellite)	4	100.0%	0.0%
6115		Technical and trade schools	3	100.0%	0.0%
Total		**All industries with IP-related revenue**	**144,259**	**100.0%**	**6.6%**

Source: ESA calculations using data from the Census Bureau's 2007 Economic Census.

Note: The intensity measure is the percent of overall revenue generated for each four-digit NAICS industry from the licensing of intellectual property protected assets.

REFERENCES

Arora, Ashish, Sharon Belenzon, and Luis A. Rios. 2011. "The Organization of R&D in American Corporations: the Determinants and Consequences of Decentralization." NBER Working Paper 17013; *www.nber.org/papers/w17013*

Bureau of Economic Analysis. 1997. *Regional Multipliers: A User Handbook for the Regional Input-Output Modeling System (RIMS II)*; *www.bea.gov/scb/pdf/regional/perinc/meth/rims2.pdf*

Cohen, Wesley M., Richard R. Nelson, and John P. Walsh. 2000. "Protecting Their Intellectual Assets: Appropriability Conditions and Why U.S. Manufacturing Firms Patent (or Not)." NBER Working Paper 7552; *www.nber.org/papers/w7552*

Hall, Bronwyn H., Adam B. Jaffe, and Manuel Trajtenberg. 2001. "The NBER Patent Citation Data File: Lessons, Insights and Methodological Tools." NBER Working Paper 8498; *www.nber.org/papers/w8498*

Hall, Bronwyn H. and Rosemarie H. Ziedonis. 2001. "The Patent Paradox Revisited: An Empirical Study of Patenting in the U.S. Semiconductor Industry, 1979-1995." *RAND Journal of Economics*. 32(1): 101–28.

Higgins, Matthew and Stuart Graham. 2009. "Balancing Innovation and Access: Patent Challenges Tip the Scales." *Science*. Vol. 326.

Interbrand. 2011a. "Best Global Brands;" *www.interbrand.com/en/best-global-brands-methodology/Overview.aspx*

Interbrand. 2011b. "Best Retail Brands;" *www.interbrand.com/en/BestRetailBrands/2011.aspx*

Jaffe, Adam and Manuel Trajtenberg. 2002. *Patents, Citations and Innovations: A Window on the Knowledge Economy*. MIT Press.

Koopman, Robert, William Powers, Zhi Wang, and Shang-Jin Wei. 2010. "Give Credit Where Credit Is Due: Tracing Value Added in Global Production Chains." NBER Working Paper 16426; *www.nber.org/papers/w16426*

Linden, Greg, Jason Dedrick, and Kenneth L. Kraemer. 2009. "Innovation and Job Creation in a Global Economy: The Case of Apple's iPod." Working Paper, Personal Computing Industry Center, University of California, Irvine; *pcic.merage.uci.edu/papers/2009/InnovationAndJobCreation.pdf*

Linden, Greg, Jason Dedrick, and Kenneth L. Kraemer. 2010. "Who Profits From Innovation in Global Value Chains? A Study of the iPod And Notebook PCs." *Industrial and Corporate Change*. 19(1): 81-116.

Maddison, Angus. 2006. *The World of Economy. A Millennial Perspective (Vol. 1). Historical Statistics (Vol. 2)*. Organization for Economic Co-operation and Development Publications.

Miller, Ronald E. and Peter D. Blair. 1985. *Input-Output Analysis: Foundations and Extensions*. Prentice-Hall, Inc.

National Economic Council, Council of Economic Advisers, and Office of Science and Technology Policy. 2011. *A Strategy for American Innovation: Securing our Economic Growth and Prosperity*; *www.whitehouse.gov/innovation/strategy*

Siwek, Stephen E. 2009. *Copyright Industries in the Economy: the 2003-2007 Report*. Economists Incorporated. Prepared for the International Intellectual Property Alliance (IIPA); *www.ei.com/downloadables/IIPASiwekReport2003-07.pdf*

U.S. Copyright Office. U.S. Library of Congress. 2009. *Annual Report of the Register of Copyrights*; *www.copyright.gov/reports/annual/2009/ar2009.pdf*

U.S. Copyright Office. U.S. Library of Congress. 2008. "Copyright Basics;" *www.copyright.gov/circs/circ1.pdf*

U.S. Patent and Trademark Office. U.S. Department of Commerce. 2010a. "Basic Facts about Trademarks;" *www.uspto.gov/trademarks/basics/BasicFacts_with_correct_links.pdf*

U.S. Patent and Trademark Office. U.S. Department of Commerce. 2010b. *Trademark Manual of Examining Procedure (TMEP)*. 7th edition; *tess2.uspto.gov/tmdb/tmep/*

White House. 2012. *Investing in America: Building an Economy That Lasts*; *www.whitehouse.gov/sites/default/files/investing_in_america_report_final.pdf*

World Intellectual Property Organization. 2003. *Guide on Surveying the Economic Contribution of Copyright-Based Industries*; *www.wipo.int/copyright/en/publications/pdf/copyright_pub_893.pdf*